D0864024

PREVIEW TO
DESTINY

A Young Girl Eases Suffering Twenty-Five Years
before God Places Her In A Role
Where Most People Prefer Not To Be.

Lauren Kirby

WESTBOW
PRESS®
A DIVISION OF THOMAS NELSON
& ZONDERVAN

WestBow Press books may be ordered through booksellers or by contacting:

WestBow Press
A Division of Thomas Nelson & Zondervan
1663 Liberty Drive
Bloomington, IN 47403
www.westbowpress.com
844-714-3454

All Scripture quotations are taken from The Holy Bible, New International
Version®, NIV® Copyright © 1973, 1978, 1984, 2011 by Biblica,
Inc.® Used by permission. All rights reserved worldwide.

ISBN: 978-1-6642-3076-7 (sc)
ISBN: 978-1-6642-3072-9 (hc)
ISBN: 978-1-6642-3073-6 (e)

Library of Congress Control Number: 2021907602

Print information available on the last page.

WestBow Press rev. date: 09/23/2021

CONTENTS

Acknowledgments.. vii
Preface ix

Chapter 1   The Little Boat 1
Chapter 2   Early Service... 3
Chapter 3   Overseas Influences 18
Chapter 4   Religious Exposure 24
Chapter 5   The Prayer for Service 34
Chapter 6   Preview to Destiny 36
Chapter 7   Dream Analysis...50
Chapter 8   Mom and Dad's Care......................................57
Chapter 9   The Mission...67
Chapter 10 Memories of Dad...85
Chapter 11 Memories of Mom..91
Chapter 12 Purpose Confirmation.................................. 107
Chapter 13 The Journey Continues 108
Chapter 14 Epilogue 110

About the Author.. 113

ACKNOWLEDGMENTS

First and foremost, thank you to the Lord for responding to my prayer and equipping me to fulfill the mission He set out for me.

To my husband and two sons, my life is rich because you are in it.

In appreciation to early readers Helga Buck, Charlotte Chere Graham, Linell Joyce, and Robin Schepper whose ideas, feedback, and recommendations were invaluable.

Thank you to Michael Kirby for the author's headshot photograph.

Thank you to the incredibly creative and talented Monica Buck Photography and Matthew Dempsey for cover photography and design.

To Rona Lafae Thappa for her insightful and candid interpretations of the dreams and their meanings.

Special thanks to Rebecca Cohen and her network through www.sharemyjourney.org and WestBow Press for bringing this project skillfully to fruition.

PREFACE

What's My Contribution?

We all wonder why we're here and what we're meant to do. What gifts were we born with? How are we intended to use them?

Over a twenty-five-year period, it became clear what my unique gifts were and how they were to be applied. From the time I was a young child and through the antics of my teen years, I was being groomed and trained for my life's work.

A plan was set in motion when I was just eight years old. I began serving and helping ease suffering long before the puzzle pieces began to fit together. After a prayer for direction, I received a series of five vivid dreams over nine years. When my eureka moment finally came, I scratched my head. *Really? Are you sure you want* me *for that? I'm such a big chicken!* Trusting the direction I had been given, I jumped into the mission and discovered a profound sense of love, mercy, and service. I'm happiest where most people prefer not to be, at a time and place we will all be one day.

I undertook work that was so much more complicated and impactful than I had ever expected, work that required much more training and hands-on experience than a short class could provide. The work involved a level of emotional intelligence and compassion that far exceeded what I believed myself capable. I wasn't in control of the curriculum or the timing. My task was and is to complete the mission chosen just for me.

You may be suspect of what you read, but I assure you, it's all true. I grappled with publishing some of the facts, but decided it wasn't my place to edit what I knew happened and was true.

CHAPTER 1

The Little Boat

There was a long, winding river with white water caps splashing along high, rocky banks. Angry whirlpools of muddy gray-green water congregated at certain points, creating downward, fast-rushing, twisting water spirals. Upstream, at the farthest end of the river, was a small boat with Brenda sitting on its floor. Her legs were crossed, and her hands gripped each side of the boat. No bench or paddles were in view. As the small, rickety boat careened around a watery bend, Brenda strained to look high up the craggy, brightly lit cliffs pointing toward the sky. She released the tight grip of one hand from the boat, raised her outstretched hand to eyebrow level, and shielded her eyes from the bright light. The return ray from the ridge was sharp and similar to the light beam reflecting the sun off a mirror. Squinting, at the top of the ridge, she saw her husband, two sons, and daughter looking down at her. No words were spoken, but there was an intense concern on both sides about how she could be so small, separating from the group, and moving swiftly down a raging river in such a small boat. Noticing whirlpools forming, a feeling of fear overtook the group, concerned that the little boat would slip into the circling force and be overtaken. Her relatives were too high and too far and couldn't help. From their vantage point, high on the sharp ridgeline, her figure looked miniscule compared to the massive, steep banks. The little boat bobbed and tossed, making its way toward the next bend. The family watched the little boat, with white caps lapping at its sides, round the last corner and bounce vicariously through gray-green water out of sight.

CHAPTER 2

Early Service
Caregiving Experiences

I was eight years old.

"Laurie!" my Mother shouted with a tone of unusual urgency. "Mrs. F. is alone and needs help with dinner and getting ready for bed. Can you go and help her?"

As a child, I would rather have been playing with my dolls or outside playing hide-and-seek.

"Where's *her* family? Why can't someone else help her? Can't *you* go?" I balked, folding my arms tightly across my chest.

"Just go! She needs help!" my Mother urged, fixing the gaze of her hazel eyes directly into my green eyes.

"OK, I'll help Mrs. F., but *The Brady Bunch* is on at eight o'clock, and I have to be home by then." I emphasized this was a need and not a want.

Mrs. F.'s arms were paralyzed and she needed help; I had to go. I wandered around the corner dragging my feet up the hill to her house and then let myself into her unlocked front door.

"I'm here, Mrs. F. Where are you?" I asked as I entered the darkened living room.

I heard a strange commotion in the back bedroom and found her on the bed. She was twisted up in a light pink nightgown, arms flailing. I couldn't tell if she was trying to put the gown on or take it off.

"Hold on! Hold on! I'm coming! Let me help you!" I said, pulling one weak arm through the correct arm hole and pulling the large open hole over her head.

"Much better!" she said. "Let's go into the kitchen, and you can make supper."

I hope she likes cereal, I thought, since I had no other meal-preparation skills. I figured the faster I did what she wanted, the sooner I'd be home and nestled in front of Marsha, Jan, Cindy, Peter, Greg, and Bobby Brady. I did my best to follow her exact instructions: get the pan, turn on the stove, put the steak in the pan, cook to medium/pink, keep some steak grease, turn off the burner, set the table, feed her, and clean up. She didn't add, "Race home by eight o'clock," so I added it to my list. At just eight years old, I had never turned on a stove or cooked a steak, medium or otherwise. I was already anticipating the adventure.

After the meal, she wasn't able to clap with appreciation, but I knew she would have if she was able. I secretly wondered how many other times she'd made the same demands, only to have the noncompliant person leave and not return. She was dominant and in charge, so if you were in her world, you had to be submissive. I walked home in the dark after nine o'clock and missed *The Brady Bunch.* This was the first of many missed shows, including *I Dream of Jeannie, Gilligan's Island, Love American Style,* and *The Partridge Family.*

As a kid, I knew about people with challenges. Living in Africa, I saw that local bakeries were host to lepers begging at the door's threshold. Patrons stepped around or over them as they entered and, on a good day, flipped one a coin. My friend in elementary school had physical challenges and could never finish the six-hundred-yard dash in the allotted time in physical education class. She always came in last, and I felt awful for her.

Mrs. F. needed help, so I rationalized that whatever she asked for, I would do.

She was a chain smoker, so she often asked me to light her

cigarette. She was famous for letting the cigarette burn all the way down to the mustard-colored filter and never dropping the ash. I noticed that her cigarette ash was now a two-inch-long gray tube curving downward, ready to break off. I was starting to feel comfortable with our new procedures. Did she need me to flick this near-dropping ash? Tipping her head in a silent "Watch me!" movement and raising her eyebrows, she turned slowly and steadily moved in toward the ashtray, like a predator approaching its prey. She kept the long ash intact and clicked her bottom teeth against the cigarette butt to flick the ash. Did she need me to extinguish her cigarette? She shook her head in a side-to-side no motion, clenched the small butt tightly between her front teeth, and held her breath. In one swift movement, she dove face-first into the filthy ashtray and smashed the butt tip against its gray base. Her face was enveloped in a thick cloud of blue smoke.

She quickly rose, inhaled a deep, fresh, satisfying breath, licked her lips, and pronounced, "You're hired!" As the remaining butt and tobacco bits smoldered (which they always did until the butt with its fuzzy white contents was half-burned, generating a putrid smell), she asked, "How would you like to be one of my helpers?" As she walked into another room, I wiped out the nasty ashtray and realized I just couldn't say no to her.

So began our five-year journey. During our time together, she taught me how to care for her: administer medications, bathe her, brush her teeth, dress and undress her, wash and style her hair, position her in bed, change her bedsheets, vacuum the living room, cook, clean the kitchen, and help her with the telephone.

Taking care of Mrs. F. was familiar to me because I previously had a life-threatening injury myself, and others cared for me. We were living in West Africa when both my parents worked for the US embassy. When I was four, I received my first pair of black patent leather shoes, likely a hand-me-down from another embassy family. They were so beautiful against the bright white of my turned-down, cuffed bobby socks. I loved those shoes. While I was wearing the shoes one day, my brother and I were racing each other by running from the kitchen wall to the sliding glass door leading to the front porch. We would touch the wall, run across the slick living room floor to the sliding glass door, touch it, and run back.

"Please, you kids, stop running in the house!" our Mother yelled. "Someone is going to get hurt!" How many times have we all heard this?

Against her wishes, we continued the race, running full speed across the room and back. On a fateful lap from the wall to the glass door, my feet tried their best to slow and brake so I could reach and touch the glass door. The problem was my body was still moving forward with the trajectory of the run, the smooth leather bottoms of the new shoes now sliding against the slick flooring. Against all efforts to stop, I crashed through the sliding glass door that led to our large, circular front porch. On impact, my right arm rose instinctively to shield my face. Until that day, my memories of being on the porch had been fond: playing with my dolls, teasing iguanas, or learning to ride my bike by pedaling around in circles for days until I mastered my balance. I landed hard on the porch. With a severe injury to my arm and wrist, I was in and out of consciousness.

My Mother wrapped my injured arm tightly in a bright white tablecloth handed to her by one of the household staff. As a Mother now, I know how small and thin a four-year-old's arm is. This injury would have covered two-thirds of the inside arm between the hand and shoulder.

I saw myself awaken in a village doctor's office. Whether this is reality or fiction, I can't say. Children process trauma much differently than adults, so I suspect, this memory is through my child's eyes. I use the term *doctor* very loosely. The setting was a round, grass-roofed hut, dirt floor, hand-hewn wooden table, and a strange elderly man hovering over me. He was no more than five feet tall and weighed about one hundred pounds soaking wet. He stood over me to inspect the wounds as the strong smell of alcohol or ether lingered in the air. He explained in French to my Mother, "Le bras doit se détacher" ("The arm must come off") at the shoulder to save my life.

Because I spoke fluent French myself, hearing this pronouncement, my adrenaline spritzed, full-body panic set in, and then my peripheral vision blended into blackness again. There's a level of regular panic and an elevated, hysterical panic you can receive when you know you're really in trouble and your life is at risk.

I experienced the latter at only four years old. Perhaps the household staff whisked me to their village doctor, and I was moved from there. There's a gap in my understanding of who did what, where, and when, but then again, I was four and unconscious most of the time.

I've since learned a more likely (and logical) scenario was that the ambassador's private plane flew me to the American base in Stuttgart, Germany. There, my arm was repaired, and I was flown home. Once home, a large, clumsy white cast encased my fingers up to my shoulder. In the African heat, the healing arm's itching was unbearable, and risk of infection elevated. Rehabilitation, archaic yet effective, involved my cutting heavy construction paper with scissors to make paper dolls thirty minutes every day. Several weeks later, one hundred and fifty stitches were removed by the embassy nurse and I had a small village of paper dolls to play with.

My new, shiny Mary Jane shoes mysteriously disappeared and were likely discarded by my Mother. I wept more for the lost shoes than for my injured arm.

Other kids didn't understand my injury, and they weren't shy about asking questions when they noticed my scars. I cringed every time I retold the story. Time and healing thankfully blended the scars into a less noticeable flesh tone. I was saved at four year's old, survived this massive injury, and my arm and fingers continue to work perfectly. The word *miracle* has been used many times to describe the ordeal.

Years later, I recounted this story to my children's pediatrician during a visit, and he said there were several reasons the accident should have either killed me or maimed me for life: in addition to my arm, my head, face, neck, abdomen, and legs should have been injured when the old-style glass shattered. The tablecloth tourniquet may have been too loose and ineffective. The time spent moving me from the porch to the hut and/or embassy for the air lift and flight time to Stuttgart delayed surgical intervention by hours, exacerbating the risk of infection or blood clots. The risk was high that all or portions of the arm and damaged areas might never again function properly.

I'd been through a life-threatening experience and become familiar with pain, fear, surgery, recovery, medical care, rehabilitation, and not being able to take care of myself. I had experienced being a patient and having caregivers. This experience was traumatic, and I'm still reminded of the accident and my recovery journey every time I see my right arm or tell the story again.

By eight years old, taking care of Mrs. F. seemed familiar because of my injury and recovery; it just wasn't where I wanted to be when my friends were playing with their dolls or outside playing kickball where I could hear their voices in the side yard.

I remember Mrs. F's hands were baby soft with fingers frozen in time, each hand in its own unique position. After so many years, it seems odd to recall her hands and fingers. This memory shouldn't surprise me though: I held her soft hands scores of times as I filed her nails the way she liked them.

Mrs. F. was a remarkable teacher, planner, and organizer. One day, she appeared in front of my fourth-grade class and announced she was the substitute teacher for the day. I was shocked! In all our time together, she never mentioned anything about being a teacher or a substitute at my school. But there she was, commanding the room, discussing assignments, and maintaining control and order. She couldn't write on the chalkboard, but she sat behind the desk or stood in front of the class with confidence and skill. She said if anyone didn't behave, she couldn't use her arms, but she sure could kick. She chuckled at her own humor, and it helped the students relax. I noted she wore the pants and blouse I laid out for her the night before, not knowing their purpose. She winked at me in acknowledgment.

On another occasion, she called me into the living room. "Laurie, I need your help. As you know, I'm the commissioner of the town's sports league."

Are you kidding me? You're the what? Nope, I didn't know!

"So," she said, "I need you to sort registration forms and checks so we can put kids on the right teams. There's a pile of envelopes on the floor."

She always said she *needed* a task to be done, eliminating any possibility of a "no thank you" response. We sat cross-legged on the carpet. I dutifully opened what felt like hundreds of envelopes and moved registration forms around the piles commensurate with the number of coaches. She talked about coaches' attributes and kids' needs and made changes to assignments. She really cared. I responded by obediently moving forms across the carpet. How she received the forms and checks and where they went next was a mystery to me.

We spent our time talking, doing chores, and enjoying each other's company. We played cards, and she beat me mercilessly at Scrabble. She'd create her words, and I placed the tiles and kept score. Or I'd hold my hand and put her cards down in front of her for her plays when we played gin rummy.

She surrounded herself with a vast network of helpers for different errands and chores, so I have no doubt I was but one of dozens of people she invited into her unique world to make it function. She never lost control or felt like a victim to her paralysis; she always found a way or solved the problems to make her world work. She was a master at making her helpers feel comfortable with what she was asking them to do. She had to; she didn't have a choice. I never heard her complain. She remained confident, driven, productive, effective, and in command of everything she orchestrated. She was mentally strong and filled with pure determination and conviction, with limitations that would have destroyed someone else.

With everything she accomplished in her life, and should have still been able to, I pondered why her arms didn't function. While Hodgkin's disease was her diagnosis, she described a wide variety of medical procedures performed in a foreign military hospital that wreaked havoc on her body. She wasn't expected to survive, so doctors tried everything in their toolbox. One surgery transferred nerves from her legs to her arms in an attempt to return function. Doctors tried varying degrees and durations of a new treatment called "radiation" to no avail. Her body was weak, but her personal constitution was fully present and engaged. She had a powerful will to live that sustained her throughout the rest of her life.

She didn't just survive. She lived as full a life as she was able and helped others thrive. She took the big bag of pithy, tart lemons she was unceremoniously given and overcame by making cold, smooth, sweet lemonade.

The last time I saw Mrs. F., it was 1982. By now, I had been married for two years and was twenty years old. I opened the still unlocked front door and entered the familiar, dim living room with my first, new son. The waft of her cigarette smell greeted me immediately.

As I settled into the couch, she asked if she could hold the baby. While I began thinking through the logistical challenges, she promptly took command, as she was known to do. She sat down on the floor with her back against the couch, her feet planted squarely on the floor, with knees up and a big smile on her face.

"Put his head against my knees with his feet against my chest," she directed me.

I placed the baby gingerly, as she requested. She nuzzled her face into his stomach and kissed his little pink bare feet and toes. She stared into his fresh face and deep blue eyes. She asked me to turn him around so she could rub her face against his fuzzy little head. I cried all the way home at the injustice of it all.

Several years later, my Mother let me know that Mrs. F. had a bad fall and was healing at home. Oh, no! She feared falling most of all. She had in-home care by then, so this was a blessing. My Mother called a few days later to let me know Mrs. F. passed away in her sleep. I was grateful that she slipped away peacefully; she experienced enough traumas in her life, and there would be something excessively unjust if this remarkable soul had a difficult passing. I attended the funeral and accepted the fresh, bright red rose boutonniere handed to me by the usher. The audience in the church was dotted with hundreds of little red roses, a tribute to persons with disabilities equality. The Father mentioned her spiritual journey and how he would miss seeing her at church.

She never let her limitations change who she was inherently meant to be: wife, Mother, teacher, commissioner, and friend. I hope to see her again when I get to heaven, and we can pick up where we left off. Maybe we'll play Scrabble, and she'll let me win for once.

I didn't know it then, but Mrs. F. gave me a wonderful toolbox filled with all sorts of tangible and interpersonal skills. Mrs. F. accepted me for who I was and made me feel mature before my time. She validated my worth and helped me overcome my insecurities. She asked about my thoughts and opinions and why I helped her. She respected me in a way I hadn't been respected before. She never treated me like a child or modified words to talk down to me. She validated that I was a smart, good, helpful, and caring person. She boosted my confidence and gave me tangible skills to care for others. She gave me comfort being around people who have real and tragic day-to-day obstacles. She allowed me to be in her innermost circle, and it was my honor. We never verbally said we loved each other, but we didn't need to. While I count her as a huge blessing in my life, I also count her as one of my greatest losses.

She donated her body to science.

Final Wishes

It was the mid 1970s when my Mother said, "Lauren, come out to the porch and let's have a talk." My thought jumped ahead: *What have I done this time?* She called me by my given name and not my nickname: not a good sign.

"There's going to come a time when your life on earth will end, so your Father and I want to talk to you about something important," she said. "Your final wishes."

"My final *what*?" I suspiciously asked, cocking my head and twisting my facial expression to show my feelings about the topic.

"There's a new organization forming to help prepare for your death and dying. Have a seat," Mom said.

"*Mine?* I'm just a kid," I said, not showing any interest and attempting to reinforce that I had places to go, people to see.

"We know, we know," she said, "but you're not promised tomorrow, so what are your wishes? For example, how about if you pick a nice dress from your closet for your burial." While still not on board with the idea, I chose a brown dress with a loosely tied bow at the neck, recently purchased for a band performance (I was the proud second-chair flute player in my middle school band; first chair eluded me).

"One more question: do you want to be cremated or buried?" my Mother asked.

Not sure exactly what being cremated involved, I said, "I don't have a preference, so you can decide."

A new hospice organization was opening, and promotional materials and education were everywhere. People who never read Elizabeth Kübler-Ross's *On Death and Dying* with its five stages of grief or thought about their own impending end were becoming educated. My Mother was like a moth to a flame. She began donating to the organization and getting serious about our family's wishes. While I understand her motivation, I'm at a loss as to why having such a conversation with a child was a good idea.

The whole concept of participating in my own or my parents' death process scared me. Mom talked about her wishes: to let nature take its course. Mom was an atheist, so she didn't have a religious basis, but she didn't want to suffer, so aligning herself with the hospice organization made sense.

Because I loved my dolls, it might be good to have them with me for eternity, similar to how the ancients were surrounded by their beloved artifacts and treasures in their tombs. I'd have to tell Mom. *I think this is a wish.* Yes, we'd been through thousands of hours of imaginative play, my dolls and I. I was there that Christmas when my favorite doll got the bright orange dune buggy she always wanted. With imaginary beaches, my doll and her friends would zip up and down my living room's sand dunes. We'd make doll houses in the snow, on tree branches, on the front porch steps, and anywhere we could find a suitable location. When all the other girls were getting large pink doll houses, I wanted one too.

"No, we don't have money for that. You'll just have to make your own," Mom said. She must have thought I would withdraw the request easily, but she underestimated me.

Tapping into a deep well of creativity and imagination, I pulled three stools out from under the kitchen table and stacked them on top of each other. Presto! A four-level home! A garage now existed under the first stool to house the new orange dune buggy, a living and dining room were set up on the second level, and an upstairs bedroom was created on the third level. Then, on the roof of the third stool (at the fourth level), I placed small furniture and created a rooftop patio for evenings and meals outside, under pretend stars. My Mother's jaw dropped as she stared at my creation. By that afternoon, she announced she wanted to vacuum and everything had to come down. Now with the prototype, the doll apartment was erected many times for hours of resourceful fun. The apartment fun ended when my Grandfather moved in with us after my Grandmother died. He was eighty-six and had dementia, and it was too risky to have my apartment building in the middle of the living room. During this time, I learned about dementia and its effects. My Grandfather hallucinated, mumbled, and was confused and forgetful.

Profound Disability

A neighborhood friend heard about a volunteer opportunity during the summer when I was fourteen. Because of Mrs. F., I was comfortable applying at a local center for profoundly disabled children. *Piece of cake. I can do this*, I thought. My years helping Mrs. F. were more than any other volunteer from my middle school had done, so I got the teacher's assistant role in the four-year-old class.

Most of the kids sat in wheelchairs and wore helmets. All wore bibs because their mouths were always relaxed and open. About halfway through the summer session, the teacher let me know that one of my little boys wasn't going to be returning to the program. He had taken a turn for the worse, so he couldn't return to my class. I had spent a lot of time with this little boy. I enjoyed playing with him, reading stories, and helping him with meals. We formed a close and trusted bond, and I would miss him. By fourteen, I had already been an active volunteer for six years and experienced caregiving and loss.

Fire Service Administration

When I was fifteen, my girlfriends and I spent hundreds of hours at the local baseball field. We dressed in Levi's cords (hip-huggers and bell-bottomed, of course, with quarter-inch-thick belt), Indian cotton shirts, and platform shoes. If it was cool outside, it was trendy to wear toe socks, each toe a different color peeking out of the open end of a fashionable platform shoe. Copying friends who were freshman cheerleaders, I often wore the traditional black-and-white saddle shoes. These were adorable with a pair of jeans or white painter's pants! As was also the fad at the time, in my back pocket was tucked a pink, six-inch long comb that remained visible about three inches. As a long-time *Brady Bunch* fan, I mimicked Marsha Brady, pulling a few strands of my very thin, blond summer hair back and tacking the limp bundle with a small barrette. I wrote to Marsha once, but to my dismay, she never responded—likely because the envelope was addressed "Marsha Brady, California." Pulling your hair back like Marsha was a big thing in the mid 1970's. Feeling quite confident and mature with my look, I spritzed my favorite perfume that smelled like baby powder from head to toe and met my friends at the ball field. Swinging our leather purses with brightly colored flower imprints, we walked up and down the sidewalk, seeing and being seen for hours on end. I looked like every other girl. Unless you had the popular ice skater's bob or famous star's long feathered bangs, you had long, straight hair, parted down the center.

Within a short time, we found our way across the street to the volunteer firehouse because we heard they had a candy machine with better candy than what ball field candy bar was selling. We began frequenting the firehouse.

One day, sitting on my friend Jean's car in the parking lot behind the firehouse, we heard a radio dispatch from the speaker secured at the back corner of the firehouse roofline. We left before the firetruck and arrived at the address first. Thinking it wise to stay out of the way and just watch, we eased beside a big, industrial-size blue dumpster. We were in position and at a safe distance. We waited for the fun to begin.

"Do you smell smoke?" I asked. She nodded.

"On that dispatch, what kind of fire call was it?" Jean asked as she put her used green Chevrolet in park.

"Dumpster fire at a commercial building, I think," said the genius sitting next to her.

We looked around to find ourselves right next to the smoking, blazing dumpster that prompted the fire call. Loud sirens blaring, the arriving units parked right next to us, blocking us in. We looked at each other aghast. With eyes wide, we dove under the dashboard and curled up like two large squirrels in a really small nest. You know how if you close your eyes real tight, you think no one will you see you? Yeah, well, it doesn't work.

Jean and I had many fun antics during our friendship. Looking back, it's nice to know that with time and maturity, we grew up and became contributing and productive members of society.

The Mother of a good friend was the president of the firehouse auxiliary, and she invited Jean and me to join. We joined officially when we turned eighteen, and I fell off my platform shoes with toe socks right into twenty years of volunteering in firehouses. We'd work bingo, run the canteen unit, organize bazaars, address banquet envelopes, organize rabies shot clinics, work annual open house events, and perform other various tasks. I spent ten years with this department and held roles such as a canteen driver, membership chair, board member, and bazaar coordinator. After my husband and I moved out of the area, I joined another department and spent almost ten years there, holding positions such as membership chair, board member, bingo manager, and president. As an adult, Jean joined another fire department after she moved away and became a certified emergency medical technician.

At seventeen, I met a young, clean-cut volunteer fireman and emergency medical technician named Pete.

"Is Lauren there?" the voice on the phone asked my Mother.

"Let me get her for you." She responded.

"Laurie! There's someone on the phone for you."

"Hi, Lauren. This is Pete from the firehouse. Some of the guys are going to the county fair, and they asked me to call you to see if you want to go."

I asked, "Who else is going?"

He assured me there would be a group going and we'd all meet at the firehouse to drive to the fair. At the appointed time, it was me, him, and one other person. As soon as we arrived, the third person walked off to meet some of his friends. In the end, it was just me and Pete, eyeing each other suspiciously.

"Look, we've set the day aside, and we're already here, so let's just do our best and have a good time," he said optimistically.

By the end of the day, we realized we had perceptions about each other that weren't true. He called again, and we began dating. We enjoyed long talks and even had the classic long walk in the pouring rain one afternoon. We stomped in puddles and laughed easily together. His extroverted personality and big laugh were infectious and served to ease my tendency toward introversion. We would sit on my parents' front porch for hours just talking about life, goals, and what we wanted to be when we grew up. He was working full-time for the police department, and I was in high school while working at a florist and an emergency veterinary clinic. We were off to a good start. He proposed that December, and we were married. May 2020 was our fortieth wedding anniversary.

I continued to serve in fire department leadership positions on boards of directors, chairs of many committees and projects, president, and board of the county fire association. In 2017 and 2018,

I served as corporate secretary for our state firefighters association. The organization was founded in 1886, and I was the first elected female executive officer. This young girl with her bell-bottoms and platform shoes actually made something of herself.

Serving to this point had been at the urging of others or total happenstance. I was learning and growing with each experience. Something good would come of it. I didn't know what, but I was sure.

CHAPTER 3

Overseas Influences

To appreciate my journey in this book, it's important to understand the upbringing and influences that impacted me as a young person.

My early years began overseas, speaking different languages, eating local flavors, and engaging in all that living abroad had to offer. These experiences shaped my view of the world with its diversity, hardships, and pleasures.

My parents met in Jeddah, Saudi Arabia, in 1958. My Father was already engaged but quickly became smitten with my intelligent, tall, slim, blond Mother. His engagement was called off, and two pairs of black onyx earrings were thrown back at him by his furious fiancée. The earrings are in my possession, and I wear them often. My parents married as 1959 came to a close and 1960 was ushered in. When their two-year assignment ended, they moved from their post in Jeddah to their next post in Beirut, Lebanon, where my brother was born. Two years later, they transferred to Nicosia, Cyprus, where I was born in an abandoned copper mine converted into a hospital.

My parents were adventurers and took advantage of the scenery, flora, fauna, and antiquity at each new post. Their tastes were eclectic, and their hobbies were varied and wide-reaching.

Entertainment consisted of lavish affairs hosted by the American embassy, roaming the landscape in search of ancient relics or fossils, and deep-sea diving in search of sunken treasure. With these many excursions, in addition to their work, my parents were away a lot, and I had feelings of abandonment.

To fit in with the locals, my Mother insisted we speak local languages, which included Lebanese, Arabic, and French spoken at home. She called me to come by saying, "Ya'ahla," or express joy with "Al hum dal'ahla." We ate rich dishes of freshly made tabbouleh and lemon- and garlic-marinated chicken called "Chicken ahla sa'hali," accompanied by homemade hummus and Arabic (pita) bread, hot off the sun's heated stone. After more than fifty years now, I can still count to ten in Arabic. I always felt different, ill-fitted in my surroundings. Consistent with my parents' prior post assignments, we moved every two years and hired locals for cooking, security, driving, and childcare. From Cyprus, we moved to Taiz, Yemen, for two years, then to West Africa, and finally to America, where my Father retired.

While my conditioning is from the posts after my birth, my most active memories begin in Ouagadougou, Upper Volta, West Africa (renamed Burkina Faso in 1984) while I was three to five years old. I lived among Africans, spoke French with the local African dialect, and my imprint was largely African. It never occurred to me that this was a unique identity and that other children weren't moving every two years, changing friends and schools, and learning a new language frequently.

My small view of this third world country consisted of our house, yard, pool, and school. When Mother would let me, I'd go with her to the local market. I remember fondly the vendors dressed in their traditional African prints of vivid red, yellow, orange, and blue offset by the strong smell of aging fish and game hung on display.

In the front yard of our home, my Mother made her best attempt to maintain the grass and other indigenous plants despite the simmering temperature. Large iguanas climbed sideways across our home's outer walls; if you startled them, they would release their tail in defense and skitter off, their hips jostling awkwardly from left to right. Acclimated to the environment, crickets and grasshoppers grew to several inches long. I remember her attempts at gardening and today enjoy maintaining several gardens myself.

My parents once hosted two European students who, in return for room and board, painted a brightly colored jungle scene on the seven-foot-high cement security wall surrounding our backyard where we played. Standout images include a huge, thick, and richly patterned snake coiled tightly around a tree, with its large, squinting eyes and striking mouth, and a vivid lion pouncing, with its claws fully extended and its mouth agape with large, sharp teeth. Light and dark green paint expertly brought indigenous trees and vegetation to life surrounding all the animals. I wonder if there are any flecks of vivid red, green, or blue paint present on the wall as the home's current occupants ponder what had been there so long ago. While invasive vines and iguanas may have taken the wall over by now, it remains bright and vibrant in my memory.

A school car drove us to school where we entered the strict environment of the all-French school, La Croix Rouge. The Madam was all business and took no guff from anyone. The Madam taught us how to read and write in French through daily assignments. Carved in our wooden desktop, an inkwell filled with shiny black liquid was ready to receive the nib of our fine, thin ink pen. A drip of black ink on one's page was viewed as failure, so we tried our hardest to control the thin pen and its ever-dripping ink between our still-developing, chubby fingers and not attract Madam's attention. At the age of four, maneuvering an ink pen under the scornful eye of the Madam was very difficult. This strict environment set in motion a deep dislike of going to school. I can say now that the Madam probably helped me respond to Mrs. F.'s commands and my service to her.

We traveled extensively by car throughout the region to explore everything Africa had to offer. My parents' adventures led us to game preserves, towering waterfalls, dry desert bush, and lush jungle.

Off-road, our little white square-back Volkswagen chugged up and down dry riverbeds in lieu of traditional dirt or paved roads. On one trip, we stood by the shore of a very muddy water hole to watch a family of alligators dive, snort, and frolic. Within moments, local village children ran toward them and in one fluid motion tossed vegetables into their open, gaping mouths. At a game preserve, our car was swarmed by curious baboons as we stopped to take in the view of the savannah. The baboons jumped on the hood of our car and sat on the windshield, caring more about the fruit they were eating than the human occupants in the car. We laughed and giggled as their bright red seats smashed flat against the glass, dramatically changing our view of the landscape.

Monsoon season would kick up violent storms and massive, regional flooding. I lay in bed one night listening to the strong winds smash the now unhinged shutters against the outside wall and rain squalls slam the roof so hard I thought the house would either implode or explode. Feelings of fear, vulnerability, and helplessness gripped me. I wanted my Mother to comfort me, but she never seemed to be home. I bonded with my nannies. The heavy rains turned once dry riverbeds used for travel into raging torrents of water and debris, blocking us in for days or weeks at a time.

The region was inherently a dangerous place for Americans lacking the necessary immune systems or encountering deadly viruses. My Father was on one of his many frequent trips and became infected with Bilharzia, a disease contracted from parasites in water. Among other symptoms, he described deep nausea, terrible aches and pains, and high fever that wouldn't break. He was deathly ill. He did eventually recover in the field and returned home thin and pale. I remember thinking, *Bill Harzia must have been a really sick and famous man because Dad's disease has his name on it.* When his new trips were announced, fear for his safety and feelings of abandonment gripped me until he returned.

The embassy was always alerting the Americans of a new virus or disease threat, which necessitated frequent shots. As a child, this was very scary and difficult for me; to this day, it takes me several days just to get up enough courage to get my annual flu shot. It took years to get up the courage to have my ears pierced.

There were many hardships and depravations in Africa. My Mother wrote to her Mother over the years, and my Grandmother kept all the letters, which are now in my possession. One April letter describes ordering flour and sugar "so the kids can have Christmas cookies." Another letter, dated February of the next year, describes sadly how the order never arrived; there were no Christmas treats, and nothing sweet had been made for months. I enjoy these letters, written in my Mother's unique script handwriting on very thin onionskin paper. I'm reminded that today's technologies with their emails and texts will no longer retain our loved one's handwriting or be available to future generations.

Leaving Africa for America, Mother traveled "light" because she was tired of depending on shipping crates that arrived broken or not at all. This included my furniture, clothes, and toys. Her solution was to give away as much as she could to the locals and get reestablished at the new location. Groggy, after sleeping for hours, I would reach my next destination with one doll and a baby blanket. Arriving at point B, there was no memory of ever leaving point A. "Où suis-je?" (Where am I?) were my first words out of the plane or helicopter. Surroundings were unfamiliar. I gripped my one doll and blanket tightly. Everything else I loved was left behind. It was time to start over again, to recover from loss again, and to be different again.

Changing conditions was a constant experience or threat to be processed. Entering a new country, I was disoriented, spoke a different language, and didn't look anything like the locals. Anxiety, grief, and loss were frequent emotions. Past friends, schools, and cherished belongings were losses to be grieved and overcome.

Some losses, experienced through sight and smell, are too painful and will never disappear. One example is the nanny who primarily took care of me and had a unique scent. I smelled it once at a mall after someone walked by in a crowd; I looked frantically for her, to no avail. Then, a corporate bathroom used the same sweet, bubble gum–scented cleaner we used in Africa; I rummaged unsuccessfully through the cupboards, trying to get the brand name. Is our house with the circular front porch still standing? How old would my nanny be now? Could she still be alive? Does she remember me, think of me?

These memories were logged as losses, and under certain conditions, they eek out of my long-term memory into my present to be grieved again fifty years later. Leaving my home for America, I had already experienced many losses: my African country, friends, toys, furnishings, clothes, primary language, and dear caregivers who took care of our home and me and my brother. Africa is where I nearly lost my life, but it was saved.

As a five-year-old child, I arrived in America during a home leave visit and later for permanent residency with feelings of insecurity, abandonment, and lack of confidence and self-esteem, not to mention a large pink scar on the inside of my right arm sure to raise attention. As we grew up, we were told to speak when spoken to and be seen and not heard. This direction was, I'm sure, prevalent in my parents' generation and how they raised their children in the 1930s and '40s, but it caused me to withdraw and feel that neither I nor what I had to say mattered. I struggled all through school as these negative self-messages slowly chewed away at the authentic person I should have become. *Would I ever find her again?* I wondered. I was a little girl who had lost her authentic voice, but over the years, through determination and professional training, I slowly regained my bearings. I am worthy; I do have something to say; I want you to listen to me.

I finally felt American and at home after discovering a link in 2018 through my Mother's ancestry to my 14-times great-Grandfather Reverend William Brewster of *Mayflower* fame. Well, if that's not American, I don't know what is! After more than fifty years, I finally found my country and felt a connection.

CHAPTER 4

Religious Exposure

B ased on the experiences to come later in this book, it's important to understand where I stood with religion after we settled in America. Up to this point, there had been no exposure.

I grew up with no real concept of the Bible or its teachings. I knew the song: Jesus loves the little children; all the little children of the world; red and yellow, black or white, they are precious in his sight; Jesus loves the little children of the world. The song was seared into my brain when I went to church with my neighbor friend Andrea at her church one Sunday. My religious awareness and journey was beginning.

The Mysterious Visitor

I was twelve. During a visit with Mrs. F., she told me a story about her ordeal after multiple surgeries and radiation treatments.

"I took pills for everything. A pill for pain, a pill to wake, and a pill to sleep," she said. "My body was so confused; it didn't know what to do. That's when I met him."

"Met *who*?" I asked, after she left me hanging with this undefined pronoun.

"I was exhausted, in pain, and hadn't slept for days. An older gentleman, dressed in crisp white, with gray hair and a kind face, came into my hospital room and walked over to my bedside. It's like he was glowing. He greeted me by name and held my pale, cold hand in his warm hands as he sat down.

"Rest now," he said as he slowly moved the hair in my eyes off to the side. "You've been through a lot, and it's time for you to close your eyes, release your fears and anxieties, let go of all this pain and suffering, and sleep. You'll feel better soon, I promise."

He sat with her, comforting her, until she fell asleep. She slept for three days. When she awoke, the pain was under control, and she felt rejuvenated, better than she had in months.

"Who was that nice man who came to see me the other day?" she asked a passing nurse dressed in the traditional white dress, cap, and shoes.

"We haven't had any visitors on this floor in weeks," the nurse responded. She checked the visitors' book. "No, there hasn't been anyone."

Mrs. F. insisted firmly, "No, there was a nice, older gentleman who came to my room and sat by my bed. He spoke to me and helped me relax and fall asleep. I know I saw him."

It was another forty years before she discovered who the kind and merciful visitor was. A new Father joined her church, and she thought he looked terribly familiar. She engaged in conversation with him after a Sunday service in an attempt to determine where she had encountered him. They couldn't initially arrive at the solution. As they got to know each other better, she unraveled the layers of her life and story. She was overseas with her husband and children and in terrible shape. She prayed in her suffering that someone would come and help her. The Father asked her what year this was, and she responded. He paused and said that very year and month, he had a religious experience that he had noted in his diary. He was praying for guidance to serve where he was needed most. The next thing he knew, he felt as though he were waking from a deep sleep. He looked at the clock, and three hours had passed. He was never able to account for the lost time. Another Father standing nearby chimed into the conversation, saying that maybe he'd been sent on a mission.

They realized that it was he who had visited her in her agony so far away, he who had prayed for her relief. The story gave me chills, and I didn't understand it. How did he get from here to there? Why didn't he know what happened? Why didn't he remember her as she remembered him? More logical questions and fewer answers.

From the Mouths of Babes

One of my earliest discussions about Christianity occurred while babysitting when I was thirteen.

"Laurie, thanks for coming over to babysit the girls. We really appreciate it," Mrs. R. said.

I'd watched these two little girls several times, and they were sweet kids. The house with its shag carpet and 1970s olive-green kitchen was always very clean and smelled of roses and a heavy cleaner. The crosses on the walls in each room did not elude me. Based on my lack of knowledge on the subject, I tried not to look directly at them, for fear their power would drop me dead. While I sat with the girls, we played with dolls, read books, and watched TV. The girls had sweet, kind spirits. After an evening of playing, I tucked the girls into their beds, turned out the light, said nighty-night, and headed for the door. Then it happened.

"Miss Laurie, can you say a prayer with us?" the elder of the two girls asked. I gulped.

"Is that, uh, something you can do by yourself?" I asked hopefully.

"No, and my Mommy and Daddy always get on their knees to pray with us," the little blond-haired, blue-eyed cherub said.

After the obvious, visible pause that was uncomfortable for all three of us, I walked over to the bed, tripped over a doll, and knelt down beside them. With my teenage frame much larger than theirs, a little cherub sat on my left, and a larger cherub sat on my right. Their little hands were clasped together, resting about halfway up the side of the mattress since they were too small to reach the top. Cherub number one, a seven-year-old, started.

"Now, I lay me down to sleep. Miss Laurie, aren't you going to pray with us?"

Cherub number two, four and a half, chimed in, "Yeah, Miss Laurie, pray with us, please! You can ask for anything, and you'll get it, like the bike I asked for, and I got it, but it was red and not pink like I asked [she gulped a breath deep into her lungs in order to continue], but that's okay because heaven heard my prayer and sent it to me for Christmas, which is when our Savior was born, and there was no place [she gulped another breath] for them to sleep, and there were animals in the room where he was born in a manger. He was wrapped in swaffling clothes." She inhaled a deep final breath in an effort to recover from her heartfelt plea for me to pray and then looked me square in the eyes.

With hesitation and under duress, I gave in. "OK, OK, I give up!" *What's happening right now? This tyke just recited the entire manger scene.* I was pretty sure I knew what "swaffling" meant, and she earned my sincere respect.

What these kids were talking about was otherworldly to me. I was raised by atheists: you can ask for something, and you either get it or you don't; then you move on. No beings other than humans were involved. Interest piqued, I wondered, *How do you pray? And what does one pray for?* So, I asked cherub number one to go ahead with her prayer. "I will really listen and then join in. I promise," I assured her. Cherub number one spoke softly in her sweet voice, a prayer that had been rehearsed every day since her life began.

They prayed in unison, "If I die before I wake, I pray the Lord my soul to take." *Oh, no, no, no. This isn't good! Nobody is dying or being taken anywhere! I'm the babysitter; could I get blamed or lose my pay?* I muttered a sincere "Amen" under my breath, hoping to contribute something recognizable that would protect me and the cherubs in my care.

When Mr. and Mrs. R. returned home, she walked across the living room to me very deliberately. I thought she was going to pay me for my night's labor with her cherubs. I mean the kids were breathing and still with us, expected to waken and not be taken.

Everyone was accounted for. At the time, fifty cents an hour was the going rate for babysitting, so I was hoping to leave with a hefty two dollars and fifty cents plus a nice tip.

"Lauren," Mrs. R. continued, "do you know who Matthew, Mark, Luke, and John are?" *She's using my given name, so I know what this means*, I thought.

Well, let me think about that a minute. Insert the *Jeopardy* tune. *Matthew was a boy at school. Mark was an American boy who lived near us when we lived in Africa, and his sister, Jennifer, was my best friend. Luke— John Wayne! No, that was the Duke. John, yes, yes, I have an answer for this one! My brother's name is Jon.*

"Yes! Got it! I know who they are," and I told her. There was a long pause, the kind that communicates extreme disappointment. Mrs. R.'s face fell.

"No, no, no, silly," she said. "From the Bible! Have you ever seen a Bible?" she said, scanning my face for the slightest hint of recognition and finding none.

She spent several minutes describing her life, how she was saved, and what she wanted and prayed for me.

These notions were new to me and gave me a lot to think about.

I said, heading for the door, "It's late, and I need to go."

Before she let me slip away, she put a small Bible in my hand. I dashed out the door with my two dollars and fifty cents plus tip and first Bible.

Over the next few months, Mrs. R. didn't forget her biblical gift and often stopped me to ask questions to see if I understood what I was reading. I was too young to connect any dots yet, but these encounters stuck with me. Eventually, when I passed by crosses in her house, I looked straight at them, pondering to myself, *What is it about you that is so mysterious? What do you mean to the world? What do you mean to me exactly? How is it possible to be three people in one? Why has your ancient symbol grown to mean so much, to so many, for so long?* Clearly, my investigative, interviewing, and analytical skills were continuing to develop. I continued reading.

Prayers for Dad

Over the next few months, my Father had significant medical issues. There were late-night trips by ambulance and surgeries to repair abdominal blockages and various-sized hernias. Late at night, he was in bed and in pain due to electrolyte imbalances.

"My legs are killing me," he would announce into the hallway for anyone in the general area. "Laurie, come here and rub my calves."

At his bedside, I'd drive a bent middle-finger knuckle into a tight spot on his calf.

"Did that hurt?" I'd ask cautiously.

"That's it," he'd say with a noise that I hoped was relief and not pain. Work on other painful spots on his calves continued until he was comfortable. I associated his problems with his excessive eating and weight. He used a large dinner plate for the main meal and the dessert. Restaurant owners trembled behind locked doors when he approached their AARP-card-carrying, 4:00 p.m. all-you-can-eat senior buffet for $1.95. I was home for dinner one evening and walked into our kitchen as he was putting all sorts of meats, vegetables, and cheeses on a large pizza.

"Oh, good. Pizza tonight," I said, eyeing two pizzas for the four of us.

"This one is for me," he said. "You, your mom, and your brother get this one."

With each illness and medical crisis, he asked for me.

"Laurie, can you bring me something to drink? I'm parched. Can you change my dressing? Your Mom isn't home, and this has to be done now. Can you sit with me a while? Can you make me a sandwich? I'm weak as a kitten."

I'd ask, "Is that warm enough? Great. Does this feel better? Good, I'm glad. Do you want cherry-vanilla or chocolate ice cream? Cherry-vanilla it is."

He was obviously in pain or incapable of helping himself, so somebody had to step in. If my Mother wasn't home, it fell to me. Mrs. F. was still in my life, and helping her was now second nature.

As with Mrs. F., I felt good when Dad let me know I'd made a difference for him. At one point, I thought I might like to be a nurse when I grew up.

As you can see, there's a lot of caregiving going on here for such a young person. There were times I felt pulled to be outside playing with friends, but when you have someone who really, really needs you for their most basic needs, you have to do the right thing and bring your best effort. I was young, but these experiences helped me grow a little bit more with each act of service.

Then the worst happened. I came home from school to find a neighbor marching deliberately across the street to meet me on my front porch. She wasn't someone I knew well, but she seemed nice enough. "Laurie, I'm so glad you're home! There's been an emergency, and your Father has been taken to the hospital! Your Mother asked me to meet you after school and stay with you until she can get home. We need to pray right now," she said with complete authority.

She grabbed both of my hands in hers and pulled the two of us down hard on the front porch step.

"Most gracious Father in heaven, please take care of Bob today as he undergoes surgery; bless the hands of everyone who works on him today."

Surgery, what? What's happening with my Dad? I thought as her words hit me and began to sink in.

She continued sincerely, "Lord, you know every fiber and cell in his body because you designed it and made it. You counted the hairs on his head. You know what's wrong and needs to be fixed; you are the great physician and healer. Lord, we pray you will heal him today if that is your will. If it's not his time to go, please send him back to us. Bless him and his family with peace and knowing that you are in control and that nothing will happen outside your will. Father, we praise you and trust that you have this situation under control. Amen. There, now doesn't that feel better? We don't need to worry anymore because we've cast our prayer," she said.

I now had a more real-life example of prayer in action. Mrs. R.

and I had been talking about philosophical situations to this point. *Is it possible this prayer could save his life?* After all, she had said, "If it's not his time to go," *go* being the operative word. Was this *go* as in "go back to his room?" Go as in leave the hospital and go home? My instincts said no, this was the real and permanent *go. My Dad could lose his life today.* I appreciated her prayer and that she was trying to make a bad situation better. She was one of my first prayer role models, and I began to appreciate what she and Mrs. R. had begun to instill in me.

He recovered after several weeks but went on to have many more bouts of ulcers, hernias, and abdominal problems. He actually died on the surgical table during his gall bladder surgery, where he later described a near-death experience during the operation. He saw himself leaving his body and entering a tunnel lined with a colored checkerboard pattern. He was asked and answered many telepathic questions about his life from a disembodied voice. The questions were transmitted into his thoughts, from which he responded. A warm, bright light at the end of the tunnel beckoned him to come. He described later that he really wanted to go, to reach the warm glow and embrace the light; however, he was told it wasn't his time, and he was thrown back. Also, he confirmed that he flat lined on the surgical table, but was revived after about forty-five seconds. He meant to write down the experience and all the questions while they were fresh in his mind, but he never did. As I considered writing this book, I was reminded that my Father never wrote down his near-death experience and all the questions he was telepathically asked during his descent down the checkered tunnel toward the light. Documenting my memories here helps ensure that future generations of my family will gain insight into my life and service. There's something cathartic about completing a task in my life that he wasn't able to complete in his.

Learning How to Pray

I now know where the authority came from and recognize my neighbor as a spiritual warrior. I even used that authority a time or two myself over the years after gaining more confidence and knowing why, when, and how to pray. I meant it when I prayed later in my life, "Lord, please heal my son's arm that he's now broken in the same place for the second time and destroyed the growth plate. Surround him with skilled and caring medical staff. You designed him and counted the hair on his head, so please protect him now." Or "Lord, protect my child as he enters college and leaves the protection of his loving, protective Mamma. Surround him with smart and caring teachers and others who want the best for him. You designed him and counted the hair on his head. Protect him and bring him home safely to me. Amen." Counting the hair placed on someone's head seemed like a very intentional thing to do for a particular reason, so I continued to add this element to the prayer; it personalized my message.

Another year, my husband had cancer, and the prayer was, "Lord, please heal the cells and tissues in his body. Come in a mighty way to keep him with us longer and give him a good life ahead. Bless the surgeons and radiologists who work with him. You designed him and counted the hair on his head, so please heal him completely, in your mighty name. Amen."

These scenarios were serious and meant something very dear to me, so I prayed sincerely for healing or survival for my loved ones. I was calling on the ultimate physician to surround and protect these real-life situations. My husband is now more than twenty years cancer-free, my eldest son graduated from college with a major in philosophy and minor in history, and my youngest son has minor effects from his twice-broken arm.

Religious Void

While raised by devout Christian Mothers, neither of my parents pursued church in their adult lives. My paternal Gandmother was Methodist and worked for a biblical society her entire career. My maternal Grandmother was an avid churchgoer too. My Mother was a confessed atheist, and my Father confessed nothing.

During family dinners, my parents would invite their friends, several of whom were Christians. They would pray before the meal. I thought it was pretty bold since they knew my family weren't Christians and couldn't fully grasp the concept of prayer. I now think it was more strategic and helped to plant seeds that could be later sown. Clearly, the seeds began to germinate with me because I'm able to recall and write about them fifty years later. I never saw a change in my parents.

CHAPTER 5

The Prayer for Service

My life up to 1985 seemed somewhat normal, at least to me. I was twenty-three; traveled extensively abroad; previously spoke Arabic, Lebanese, and French; almost had my right arm amputated; was a babysitter, caregiver, and teacher's aide; was married for five years with a three-year-old son; worked at a government contractor with a high-level security clearance; and was a member of the firehouse auxiliary. Looking back, I realize this isn't so normal for a twenty-three-year-old.

While serving in many volunteer roles, I still didn't feel fulfilled. It was getting harder to get up in the morning and drag myself in for a volunteer assignment. Gifts and abilities were right under the surface, revealing hidden traits every now and then. Skills were slowly being revealed in my professional work, but I began searching for the gifts that would feed my soul and serve the larger community. After attending a local church with a neighbor, I answered the altar call and was saved on a sunny Sunday morning. The baptism that followed was thrilling, and my religious journey was well underway.

After fully immersing in the church and a local Bible study, I became aware that many of my friends at church and in the home group spoke of their missions. I wondered what my mission was and where I was supposed to serve. Praying was now a much more common practice, so I prayed: "Lord, you know me. You designed me and counted every hair on my head. You gave me gifts. Please reveal them and direct me to where you need me to be, doing what you need me to do. You've probably given me hints that I've missed; sorry about that. Please show me again where you would have me serve your kingdom. Send me where you need me the most. Amen."

With my prayer in place, I waited for the reply, not quite sure what shape it may take. When His response began to unfold, I was stunned. No way did I think, under my own power, I could fulfill the mission He set out for me. My life and the lives of many others would never be the same.

CHAPTER 6
Preview to Destiny

After my prayer asking for clarity and direction, I had a series of five dreams over nine years. What follows are true descriptions of what happened before, during, and after each dream. Names and some details have been changed to protect the identity of the dream subject. With each dream, the puzzle pieces came closer together to form a complete picture.

Dream 1—Unnamed

It was December 1985. I was twenty-three. The dream opened with a bathtub filled with water. The water was murky, as though someone had already bathed, creating a thin, soapy film on the surface. Bobbing to the surface with buoyancy floated a small, pale figure hidden behind a thin veil. The veil was more like a translucent sac versus the soapy water's film. Palms up, two large hands rose from under the water under the little being's back and broke the water's surface. In a smooth scooping motion, the little being was raised up and nestled in the palms of the large hands. The once-filled veil emptied, leaving the little figure still covered but more defined. There was an overwhelming sense of stillness, and the dream ended.

I awoke shaking, my heart racing, not sure what I had just experienced. The images were clear with distinct, identifiable detail.

No emotions from the hands' source or the little being were emitted to me during the dream or afterward.

A few days later, it was Christmas Eve. I hadn't felt well all day. I was crampy and achy and not comfortable when I went to bed.

"At fourteen weeks' pregnant, I shouldn't feel this way," I told my husband.

I should have started wearing maternity clothes by then but wasn't. A call to the doctor confirmed that either the fetus was pressing on a nerve or a miscarriage was imminent. I prayed for the pregnancy to be saved.

In the wee hours of Christmas morning, the pregnancy ended. I cried that my pregnancy was over and that what should have been a baby in a few months was not to be. Every June 21, my due date, I say a little prayer. No longer pregnant, we faced Christmas morning with our three-year-old son.

We pretended to have a good time and give our son a great Christmas. We'd been up all night, but he didn't know. He tore through the boxes and contents. Preferring boxes over the gifts, one box immediately converted into his own private airplane. I made a mental note to spend more time looking for strong boxes and spending less money on actual gifts in the future. When it was my turn, there was a large box under the tree from my Mother. I gently pulled back the stark white tissue paper. Underneath, neatly folded, was a wide array of handmade, colorful maternity outfits.

Later in the day, after the night and day's events calmed down, it hit me. I had that strange dream about the bathtub and the little being just three days before. I was still processing the dream and unclear what it was about.

This dream exposed me to sudden death and the notion that life is not time bound; a higher power decides if and for how long we each live. And, if the journey begins, it can change; what was meant to be may no longer be meant to be. My faith allowed me to be comforted even though I didn't have all the answers.

Dream 2—Pam

It was June 1986. The dream opened with my relative Pam, her husband, and their children on the left bank of a narrow, wet gorge. While water wasn't visible, there were dark remains as if water had recently been present. Bronze-blue clouds indicated it was just about dusk. I could see each person clearly; they were huddled together tightly with their arms around one another. Then Pam slowly started to separate herself from the group and take a few steps forward. Her family called out to her, urging her not to go. She walked toward a narrow gulf, hastening her pace. She looked back over her shoulder again to see her family. Feeling a quickening sense of urgency, she approached the bank and could barely make out the familiar features of her Mother and Father on the other side. She moved forward, looking over her shoulder one more time. With one step over the gulf, there was a flash of light, and Pam was instantly transported to the opposite shore. Before her feet hit the ground, she transformed into a little girl wearing a party dress. Her dark hair was pulled back with a big pink ribbon, and a large bow was tied at the back of her dress. She wore white bobby socks and shiny, black patent leather shoes. She appeared to be about five years old. She ran fast toward her Father, who knelt to receive her. She leapt into his outstretched, welcoming arms. He smiled broadly as he wrapped his arms around her and lifted her to his chest in a huge, loving bear hug. There was a feeling of pure joy to be reunited after such a long separation.

I jerked awake, not sure why my relative and her family were so prominently in my dream. In the prior dream, the little being wasn't identifiable. What did this mean? Again, the details were just as vivid as the prior dream. The bright color of the ribbons and shiny black Mary Janes were similar to mine in Africa. Conflicting feelings of longing, sadness, loss, release, anticipation, and joy invaded my thoughts and heart. Pam's earthly family was losing her, and there was great sadness; her heavenly family was receiving her, and there was great joy and excitement. My relative felt sad as she walked away and looked over her shoulder but accepted it was her time; she was excited to see her parents and elated to make the crossing into the waiting arms of her Father. These emotions carried from the dream to me.

Should I mention this to my husband? I did, and he was just as baffled as I was.

I decided to take a chance and write to my relative's husband to let him know about the dream and that his wife was a fine, beautiful, vibrant little girl in the loving arms of her parents. I wrote the letter quickly before changing my mind. Adding his address and a stamp, a standing mailbox was found to receive my envelope so I couldn't back out.

I shouldn't be afraid, I thought. Justifying that my experience was real and true, I felt it was the right thing to do, and the letter went off.

"Laurie, I got some sad news today. Pam passed away," my Mother said.

It was the third day since my dream, but I said nothing. It was also six months since my last dream. *What a coincidence. What's going on here?* I told my husband, and we looked at each other in disbelief.

My relative was a very kind and peaceful soul. She was my Mother's closest confidante. She had been diagnosed with cancer a year or two before. Unfamiliar terms such as "small cell," "lymph node involvement," and "metastasized" were used to describe her condition.

Our family attended her funeral service, but my letter wasn't mentioned. Everyone spoke well of the hospice organization and hospice nurse involved in her care. I was glad my relatives were surrounded by people who had the knowledge, skill, and ability to help in their time of need. Caring for people for sixteen years at this point, I knew what it took to be in the details of someone's daily life and long-term ailments. Still fearful of her husband's response, I secretly hoped the envelope would be lost in the mail. About a week later, he called to say that he read the letter. He said it gave him a sense of comfort about where his beloved wife had gone, peace knowing she wasn't in any pain, and happiness that she was with her parents. His response was so positive and kind; the letter had been received as intended, and my anxiety faded.

This was my first experience with hospice care apart from my Mother's discussion with me years before.

Pam's death exposed me to a cancer patient under hospice care who accepted the terms of her passing. I became aware that the hospice nurse and hospice philosophy played a huge role in her end-of-life experience.

Dream 3—Brenda

I was now twenty-eight with eight- and three-year-old sons; it was March 1990. My second son was born healthy in 1987 and, yes, I was finally able to enjoy my Mother's maternity clothes. Exhausted after a day's work, making dinner, managing homework, and putting kids to bed, I was looking forward to a good night's sleep.

The scene came into view. There was a long, winding river with white water caps splashing along high, rocky banks. Angry whirlpools of muddy gray-green water congregated at certain points, creating downward, fast-rushing, twisting water spirals. Upstream, at the farthest end of the river, was a small boat with Brenda sitting on its floor. Her legs were crossed, and her hands gripped each side of the boat. No bench or paddles were in view. As the small, rickety boat careened around a watery bend, Brenda strained to look high up the craggy, brightly lit cliffs pointing toward the sky. She released the tight grip of one hand from the boat, raised her outstretched hand to eyebrow level, and shielded her eyes from the bright light. The return ray from the ridge was sharp and similar to the light beam reflecting the sun off a mirror. Squinting, at the top of the ridge, she saw her husband, two sons, and daughter looking down at her. No words were spoken, but there was an intense concern on both sides about how she could be so small, separating from the group, and moving swiftly down a raging river in such a small boat. Noticing whirlpools forming, a feeling of fear overtook the group, concerned that the little boat would slip into the circling force and be overtaken. Her relatives were too high and too far and couldn't help.

From their vantage point, high on the sharp ridgeline, her figure looked miniscule compared to the massive, steep banks. The little boat bobbed and tossed, making its way toward the next bend. The family watched the little boat, with white caps lapping at its sides, round the last corner and bounce vicariously through gray-green water out of sight.

"Every time I bend over, there's an incredibly sharp pain at the back of my head," Brenda confided, holding the base of her skull one night during a visit.

"That's not right," I said. "You need to get that checked."

She did, and after all the tests, it was confirmed that she had cancer. It was later confirmed to be lung cancer metastasized to the brain. She completed chemotherapy, lost her hair, and remained strong. One evening, she asked me to sit with her. She was lying on the couch with her favorite scarf covering her head. I noticed her favorite stuffed animals keeping guard at the far end of the couch as I sat cross-legged by her on the floor.

"What do you think heaven will be like?" she asked me.

I tried my best not to change expression as I prayed, *"Lord, if you're there, it's me. I don't know what to say right now. Please give me the words you would have me say. I need your help!"* I collected myself, paused, and continued.

"Well," I began slowly, "I think it will be full of light, peace, and beauty. There won't be any more pain, suffering, illness, or hatred."

She said, "I think that sounds nice."

"Thank you," I quietly whispered under my breath.

Hospice was called in, and the nurses and nursing assistants helped the family through the unfolding processes. They followed their standard protocols to set up the room and bed, store certain supplies and medications, educate Brenda and the family, keep the family informed, and determine how much support would be needed. They made a difference. "You are angels on earth," I told them on the driveway one evening, after a particularly difficult visit.

"You should come. We think it's almost time," said the voice on the phone. This scenario played out many times over the next few weeks. The family would arrive ready for the worst, and it didn't happen. Brenda had good days and not-so-good days. A few days before she passed, I had the dream described above. On the last day, a beautiful spring day in March, she passed peacefully, surrounded by her family. I remembered our discussion on the couch, hoping she gained comfort for what was now unfolding. I hoped her spirit was now free to fly to the light- and love-filled place. Brenda was on her way.

These dreams were now a trend, and it was the third day, four years since the last dream.

This dream exposed me to a cancer patient with hospice care and my praying for the words to say.

Dream 4—Andrea

It was April 1993, and I was now thirty-one. In my deepest sleep, the dream opened with voices.

"I'm not going in there, and you can't make me," a childlike voice demanded of the large, warm beam of light in the pool.

"Come in. The water is nice and warm, and I will catch you," the presence urged without using words.

"Nope. Not going to do it," Andrea said firmly, shaking her head from side to side.

"Just put a toe in, and you'll see. Everything is good here, and I will make sure you're safe," the presence said calmly.

After an extended pause, Andrea thought long and hard. She put her toe in, and it was good. She pulled it out quickly, not wanting to be fooled.

"See? You can do it," the deep voice encouraged. "Just jump in, and I'll catch you."

"I'm not ready yet," Andrea said.

"I can wait for you. There's no rush. I was here the day you were born. I've always been here, and I will be here the day you die," the disembodied voice comforted.

Andrea stood firm and wasn't going anywhere. She rationalized that she could stand and wait for the inevitable or take this leap of faith and jump into the water with the yet unnamed presence.

"I'm too young, and this shouldn't be happening to me! I can't go yet," she pleaded.

Based on her experiences, she knew the pool should be filled with water; what she actually saw was light. She dipped her toe in deeper, and it was still good. She was perplexed how she found herself in this position. There wasn't a sense of fear as much as a sense of bewilderment. At just thirty-one, with a new husband, job, life, and children ahead of her, how could she be face-to-face with this presence asking her to jump into a pool that wasn't water but really light? What she did know was that she wasn't afraid of the pool, and she wasn't afraid of him. There was something familiar about his presence and energy, and she'd felt it before. She moved back and forth between feelings of denial and acceptance. After weighing all her options, she reached a point where she felt strong enough.

"I have to go. What choice do I have left?" she concluded.

Her back was against an unmoving wall, and all options had been exhausted. Andrea closed her eyes, released all her fears, and slipped into the waiting arms of warm light. Her slow entry into the pool and below the surface was punctuated by rings of ripples across the water's sun-lit surface. The final setting was peaceful as Andrea and the lit spirit water melded into one.

I woke in the morning, aware of the dream but not in the familiar state of terror. This dream was different; Andrea became ready to go. She reached a state of acceptance and released herself with confidence into the light.

Andrea was my first friend on the block when we moved to the US after a life overseas. She was in my first-grade class, and we made each other laugh easily. We also got into some mischief together. In second grade, we learned there was a soda machine in the teachers' lounge at our elementary school. With twenty-five cents saved from our lunch, we decided to go into the lounge and buy a soda. We found the machine, inserted our quarter, pressed the button, and grabbed the glass bottle as it clanked down into the waiting metal tray. Then it happened: high-heeled shoes were coming toward us, clicking on the hard floor. We scampered around a corner into a small separate room that served as the teachers' seating area. Andrea and I hid. The clicking shoes grew louder.

With a final click followed by marked silence, the teacher stood inside the lounge, scanned the room, and walked toward the seats. She saw me first. "Get out from behind there! You're in a world of trouble, young lady. Wait until your Mother finds out!"

In one swift movement, she reached toward me, and her long, red-painted fingernails grasped my upper arm tightly. She pulled me out from behind the couch. Turning to leave with me securely anchored, she noticed Andrea hunkered down beside a shelf. She lifted us both off the ground, our feet struggling to connect with the floor, and marched us down the hall and up the short flight of stairs. Our prized possession, the soda bottle that made the risk worth taking, was left beside the shelf where Andrea had huddled.

A wooden sign with gold trim nailed to the door announced to anyone in the area, "Principal's Office." Once inside, we were ushered to sit in front of a large, wide desk and an angry principal. The teacher stood inside the door, crossed her arms, and explained our transgressions to the judge, jury, and executioner. She angrily tapped out the now-familiar click of her high-heeled shoe impatiently. In the principal's office, we were admonished for entering the exclusive lounge, off-limits to students. After being given a strict lecture about staying out of the teachers' lounge, we were given handwritten notes about our crimes we were to give to our parents as soon as we got home from school. We lumbered back to our classrooms, each with notes tucked in our pockets for our respective parents. In our young minds, we just wanted a soda and didn't mean any harm. Was our approach creative? Yes. Did the adults think so? No.

When we were twelve, Andrea invited me to go to her church summer camp for ten days. Again, my familiarity with anything related to church was minimal, but the chance to get away from home for the first time and into the woods seemed like fun. We sang Christian songs that were unfamiliar to me, ate oatmeal with prunes every morning, swam in the pool, played games, and had a great time.

"Oh Christ, thou Lamb of God, who taketh away the sin of the world. Grant us thy peace," we sang. I liked the tune, and the words stuck with me.

"Sure you can come for a visit, but Andrea doesn't look like what you remember. She's in a wheelchair now, has lost weight, and is in a lot of pain," her Mother said when I inquired if my childhood friend was up for a visit. Arriving on the appointed day and time, I bent over to give her a gentle hug and noticed that her nails were long with a perfect French manicure.

Andrea suffered from severe back pain, and treatments given for a year provided no relief or resolution. The pain was worsening by the time it was decided everything that could be done was being done. Andrea sought a second opinion, and a battery of tests confirmed she had cancer that was widespread. Like me, she was thirty-one. Learning her fate, she and her fiancé hastened their wedding. Andrea gingerly rose from the wheelchair and walked down the aisle arm in arm with her Father as a long white veil followed her steps. I prayed that the adrenaline generated from the day's events would numb her pain. Reaching the altar, she was slowly lowered back into the wheelchair. After the ceremony, she was raised from her wheelchair again, transferred, and lowered into the waiting black limousine. She was beautiful in her white dress and veil, accentuated by her dark hair, porcelain skin, and deep blue eyes. I noted how her full veil, once fully tucked in around her, consumed the back seat like fluffy white clouds.

There was no doubt that it was Andrea in the dream and what the warm light represented. In the dream, Andrea was negotiating back and forth with the light. This negotiation, from what I learned from her disease, may have played out in the hospital. Eerily, the feelings in the dream could have matched what she experienced in her real-life struggle.

The presence in the pool definitely felt and sounded male; it had a kind voice, was patient and respectful, and waited for Andrea to reach a comfortable place on her own to let go. The voice described being there the day she was born, always being there, and that it would be there the day she died.

"Andrea's gone," said my friend from elementary school during a phone call. "She died today, and I just talked to her Mom."

She shared the details on our call. It was the third day since the dream and three years since my last dream.

It was early spring, and Andrea's funeral service was held at the church in our town where she grew up, where I attended my first church summer camp when we were twelve, and where she was married. Familiar friends from the old neighborhood were there, and old stories were recounted. Then I wept openly in the pew and couldn't pull myself together. With black smudges under my eyes, I admonished myself for wearing mascara to a funeral.

As I blew my nose for the last time, I tucked the tissue into my purse, walked out of the church to my car, and drove away.

This dream exposed me to a cancer patient who was not ready to die and used every possible technique to change the outcome of her death, all the while the male light form waited patiently for her to let go. *How kind and merciful*, I thought.

About a year after Andrea died, she appeared in a vivid dream where there was a large party and many people pressed tightly against one another in a room not large enough to hold them. Looking over the heads of partygoers, I saw Andrea at a far distance, moving along a back wall. Her dark hair was down around her shoulders, and her vivid blue eyes leapt from her fair skin and shone across the room. She was wearing a bright emerald-blue taffeta gown that matched the color of her eyes. It was a vivid and unique shade of blue that I have no words to describe. She saw me from the distance, and we made eye contact. Our stare lasted a moment as I tried to signal for her to come over to me. She kept gliding along as if caught up in a current of people from which she couldn't extract herself.

Her gaze seemed to say, "I see you, old friend, but I can't get to you. There's a great distance between us now. I am in a hurry and need to move along with the others."

Dream 5—Sandy

It was 1994, and I was enjoying a good sleep. I saw a small plane flying high over a vast ocean, its wings teetering in the winds aloft. Several jumpers looked through the small windows at the teeming ocean below. Each contemplated all the moves needed to successfully jump out of the plane, deploy their parachutes, and make a safe landing.

"OK, on three, everybody moves down the line to jump," a deep male voice announced through the on-board speakers.

A woman toward the back of the line had a frozen hand gripping the parachute release cord. She felt fear rising from her chest and heating her face; her heartbeat quickened.

"I don't want to go. I can't go," she said out loud to no one listening.

There were several jumpers on the plane moving toward the open door, and nobody acknowledged her presence. They were on their own journey. Sweat formed on her upper lip and brow as she began to feel the physical effects of her anxiety. The others were silent as they jumped one by one, the wind from the open door filling the cabin. She was tens of thousands of feet high, embedded in a line of jumpers, and there was no backing out. *This was happening.*

The jumper ahead of her leapt. With the prior jump complete, she was jerked forward, yanked by the line to the opening. She fell, arms outstretched, mouth open, releasing a silent gasp that started in her throat but never left her mouth. She struggled to get her bearings and put her hand back on the parachute pull cord.

"I don't want to go! I can't! I'm not ready!" she released into the wind.

She finally found the parachute pull cord and gave it a hard yank, hopeful it would save her. Nothing happened. She pulled again harder. Still nothing. She was now in a free fall, headed straight for the teeming ocean below. She gasped, trying to breathe, but the wind was blowing hard right into her face, and she couldn't catch her breath. She struggled to move numbing fingers to find the backup parachute's pull cord. Her hands stopped working, and her brain no longer commanded her fingers what to do. Her arms and legs flailed, ripping at her jumpsuit as she moved her hands up and down, trying to find a cord for help. Her head was the heaviest part of her body, so her weight shifted, and the top of her head now faced the fall full force, her body now trailing. In a moment of acceptance, she relaxed, fully ready to let go. The space between the plane and the ocean narrowed as her body sped toward the water's choppy surface with small whitecaps dotting the low waves. She looked around one more time for any last source of help. Seeing none, she resolved that this was the end. Her life hadn't been perfect, but it was uniquely hers, and she had no regrets. She was devoutly Jewish and committed to her faith. She closed her eyes and entered the water. Was she alive? She broke the water's surface, squinted toward the shoreline, and found small images of people she recognized as her family. She tried to move and swim.

I'm alive but no longer whole, she thought as she slowly and gingerly swam forward. She wasn't in any pain.

She swam slowly, moving only her arms in broad outward strokes, her chin lifted out of the water. About fifty yards offshore, she slowed her swim, recognized the figure on the shore, and made eye contact with her husband.

Her husband ran toward the shore. "You made it. You're okay, so come onto the shore and let's go home," he said.

Sandy pondered her answer for a moment. "I can't," she said slowly. "I need to stay here."

Confused by her response, her husband begged her to come again. "Just swim a little more, and I'll come out to meet you," he urged.

"No," she said, "that's not possible. It's over, and I have to stay here."

Pleading and begging, her husband broke down in tears on the shore and dropped to his knees. Without another word, she made eye contact with her husband one more time, holding her gaze and searing his features from her short- into her long-term memory. She used her arms to turn slowly and made her way back out to sea.

I have memories of her visiting our home as I was growing up. She and my Mother had coffee on our screened-in back porch, where she became a target for my pet squirrel. This hairless, squirmy, and tiny pink little fellow was about the size of an adult-size thumb when I found him after a storm under the large oak tree in our front yard. *His nest must have toppled*, I concluded. He was presented to my Mother, who tucked him in a box. The next morning, she visited the local pharmacist, who recommended feeding him thinned baby cereal through an eye dropper. We named our new hairless friend Earl the Squirrel and announced to Mother that we were keeping him. Earl rode in my shirt pocket for the next few weeks as he gained his strength and grew a complement of fur from nose to tail. During one visit when Sandy sat at the table on the back porch, Earl sniffed the air, identified an interesting target, and immediately hopped on Sandy's leg. Within a few moments, I heard the commotion: Earl bit Sandy. From then on, Sandy and Mom had their coffee in the kitchen.

"Laurie, you remember my friend Sandy, right?" Mom asked.

"Sure, I remember her; she was Earl's friend," I said, deploying my best attempt at being clever (which she never appreciated).

Well, she had liver disease and has been very sick. She let me know Sandy passed away. My attempt at humor was ill placed. I hadn't seen Sandy for a few months, but we did talk on the phone once. "You'll get old like me someday, but you know what, Laurie? As long as you have your health, you'll be okay," she told me.

I said, trying to recover from my comment, "That's too bad about Sandy. She was a nice lady. I'm sorry you lost your friend."

At first, I didn't make the connection between my dream and Sandy. My recent dream didn't clearly identify the parachutist. After recounting the details of the dream, with what I knew about Sandy's personality, temperament, and tone of voice, I resolved that it was, in fact, Sandy. I felt her in my bones. Feeling vulnerable with her own aging and physical ailment were the exact sentiments she shared with me the last time we spoke. It was the third day, one year since the last dream.

This dream exposed me to a long-term illness and a strong-willed patient who wasn't ready to go and never reached acceptance. This last dream was the most intense of the five dreams over a nine-year period.

CHAPTER 7

Dream Analysis

We all have dreams or visions, but do they have meaning or serve a purpose? Are they intended to simply occur and fade, or are they a call to action? Dreams and visions are frequently described in the Bible. These excerpts describe visions and dreams similar to my experience:

- Acts 2:17 (NIV): "In the last days, God says, I will pour out my Spirit on all people. Your sons and daughters will prophesy, your young men will see visions, your old men will dream dreams."
- Job 33:14–15 (NIV): "For God does speak—now one way, now another—though no one perceives it. In a dream, in a vision of the night, when deep sleep falls on people as they slumber in their beds."
- Daniel 7:1 (NIV): "In the first year of Belshazzar king of Babylon, Daniel had a dream, and visions passed through his mind as he was lying in bed. He wrote down the substance of his dream."

During the months and years between my dreams, life moved along. I worked full-time, volunteered, took care of my two children, read, did arts and crafts, worked in my gardens, and went to church and the grocery store—just normal, everyday life. With each dream, I hoped it would be the last because they and the subject's passing on the third day was disconcerting. The resurrection occurred on the third day, and that's all I could connect to the third day in my dreams. Below are biblical references to the third day:

- Luke 24:7: "The Son of Man must be delivered over to the hands of sinners, be crucified and on the third day be raised again."
- Hosea 6:2: "After two days he will revive us; on the third day he will restore us, that we may live in his presence."

Had I caused the deaths? No, their death and dying journey was already ordained and underway; I was an observer, given a preview. I was determined to figure out the purpose for the five dreams because I didn't feel they were haphazardly brought to me.

Below are some common features of the dreams:

- Five dreams spanned nine years, separated between one to four years. The dreams occurred when they were intended to further my development and appreciation for how end of life can unfold, so I could apply what I learned to my mission.
- Specific details were vivid and colorful. Colors were crisp, bright, and nothing like I've ever seen, colors I have no words to describe.
- Emotionally charged feelings, when present, transferred from the main and supporting actors to me. Every emotion, it was clear, had a purpose that I was meant to feel.
- Subjects in the dreams became recognizable to me either physically or through feelings. For the Unnamed, I didn't know the identity until the miscarriage on the third day.
- Water or an implication of water was a prominent feature in or near a gulf where water was passing or had passed between two sides.

- Light was predominant in three of the dreams.
- Hospice care was provided to the subjects (Pam and Brenda) of two dreams; based on the availability of hospice services at the time, it is highly probable that two other dream subjects (Andrea and Sandy) had hospice care.
- Emotions in each dream dialed up in intensity from none (dream one), more (dream two), even more extreme (dreams three and four), then to the most extreme (dream five).
- There was no presence or implication that anyone in the dreams was in any pain.
- No emotions were transferred to me during dream one, the miscarriage. This was merciful considering it was my very own experience, and I did grieve the loss after it occurred.
- Each dream provided exposure and experience to varied forms of death experiences. Each expanded my sense of empathy, caregiving, communications, and understanding of the death and dying process for the person passing and those left behind.
- While it was mysterious that these dreams were communicated after my prayer, it was most mysterious about the subject's passing on the third day and if/how this paralleled with the resurrection. This meaning still confounds me, and when I get to heaven, I'll be sure to ask about this.

Obviously, dreams that shake you awake are intense. From the age of four, I suffered from nightmares after my arm injury and life experiences living abroad. Some dreams are so intense they not only wake you but cause you to get up for a drink of water and attempt to clear your head before climbing back in bed. Dreams can wake you, shaking, panting, and sweating, or calm, reflective, and pensive. You might wake with your eyes wide open or sit up straight in bed. They may leave you wanting more or praying this particular type of dream will end and never recur. My dreams began slowly, each dream more intense than its predecessor. My feelings and reactions were those of the main or supporting actors in the dreams. The dreams strengthened my fortitude and were rehearsals for my mission yet to be revealed. There were now many puzzle pieces to fit together.

In all five dreams, the visual details were studied to review what happened during the dream and the emotions that transferred to me. How did I feel before, during, and after each dream?

- Dream 1—Unnamed: The little being's existence was very brief—not meant to be, not this time, not now. The large hands that cupped the little body were those of its maker, deciding to take the being back from whence it came. This wasn't a mistake, just a shift in direction; the little being was needed elsewhere. While tragic, it felt as though the entity associated with the hands was simply taking it back for a different purpose. No specific emotions were transferred to me during the dream, and I rest in the peace that it wasn't meant to be and we will be reunited someday.

- Dream 2—Pam: While Pam didn't want to go, she understood it was her time and felt ready. This dream was about acceptance and facing death with a sense of peace and readiness. Her dream introduced emotions of sadness, acceptance, release, and crossing over with grace and joy. Had she accepted that all possible medical interventions available had been done? Had she come to accept her passing? Had her dedication to her church and knowledge of biblical ideologies given her peace, knowledge, and readiness for what was to come? Had the hospice staff educated her on the death and dying process, preparing her for the stages sufficiently enough for her to accept it and face it without fear? I know so.

- Dream 3—Brenda: Moving along turbulent waters, Brenda felt a sense of the widening separation from her family on the ridge, but there wasn't a fear. She accepted what was happening and went along after realizing nothing else could be done. While in other dreams, the emotions came from the subject, in this dream, the emotions came most predominantly from the onlookers: her family on the ridge. Her husband, two sons, and daughter felt their own emotions based on what Brenda meant to them. The family emanated their feelings to hold on tightly. In this dream, the family was more fearful and trying more to keep control of the uncontrollable than Brenda herself. She reached a place of acceptance ten months after diagnosis. During that time, she continued to love her husband, children, and grandchildren. Raised in a Christian home and singing in a family group, were there memories of biblical teachings and life after death? Did her hospice team help her and her family in this understanding and transition? On the day she asked me about heaven, she accepted the response with a peaceful smile. I hope she had a vivid image of heaven when she passed. I believe she was at peace when she left her mountaintop log cabin and transported to a new beginning filled with light and love.

- Dream 4—Andrea: Andrea fought hard to stay, and acceptance of her passing was reached only in the last brief instant. For this vibrant thirty-one-year-old, her death felt like an injustice, and she had significant regrets. There was no family observed as part of her dream: Andrea appeared as a child alone at the pool's edge. She worked through her emotions, options, and acceptance alone. When she made her decision after deep deliberation, she acted on it with confidence. My longtime friend was in disbelief that her cancer was actually going to take her. I don't know if she had hospice care, but by this time, it was certainly well established in our community. She fought to stay, fought to live. She negotiated with the notion of the end. She processed the pros and cons, the whys and why nots. She couldn't go back and didn't like this notion of stepping into the unknown pool with its voice encouraging her to step in. She had no choice but to take a leap of faith and dip her toes in slowly, confirming this was really happening and now was her time—not tomorrow or today but now. She reached acceptance only when she had processed everything there was left to process, and then she released her spirit. The being that helped her through the process was a male voice that gave her comfort; it was patient and received her when she was ready. She had no choice but to trust the brightly lit pool, a feeling I believe she was already familiar with based on her upbringing.

- Dream 5—Sandy: Sandy fought hard to stay and live another day. Accepting her passing didn't come easily. She tried to control her own outcome, and it just wasn't possible. She had no control; her experience was unfolding. She was facing her own death and was in denial until the very end. She didn't accept her fate until she was in the water facing her husband and accepting that she had to live in another place. The intensity of the dreams was now at its height with Sandy's passing. She eventually resigned to her fate as she slowly swam away to another place. All of Sandy's feelings transferred to me during the dream.

Through my own process of analyzing and understanding each experience, I reflected on my responses. After all, these experiences were brought to me for a reason and I now had to live with them. While I've lived with them for many years, telling my story through this book is part of my journey.

The dreams were visited on me, I believe, for a wider purpose. My overwhelming conclusion is that I was given a view into the death and dying process and how to recover afterward. Deeper still, experiencing the emotions involved as death and dying unfolds equipped me to talk with people about the experience. My only knowledge about death and dying up to this point was my Mother's connection to our local hospice organization many years earlier and her awkward request for my final wishes.

By 1995, I experienced the passing of friends and relatives. My friend in seventh grade died when her mini-bike flipped (the same one she and I had been on a week earlier). This hit close to home, as I could easily have been on that bike. My parents were in their late thirties when I was born, and their parents and extended family were older. By 1985, most of them were gone. Losses were experienced during my life abroad in Saudi Arabia and Africa. While not physical death, loss comes from separation, longing for something or someone you will never see again. I resolved to watch for signs about death and dying to further unravel the clues. During this time, I became fascinated about where this trip would lead and what role I was to play.

I remembered my prayer from years earlier when I asked for clarification of my gifts and where to serve. Struggling with the meaning of the dreams, I prayed for clarity.

"Lord, I believe the dreams were sent to me for a reason, and they are your reply to my request for guidance where I should serve. After reviewing and analyzing all the dreams, I could really use your help to understand what it all means. Amen."

My thoughts received this: "I've equipped you through different scenarios and shown you where I want you to be. I've prepared you to serve the dying where there is great suffering."

Then, in an instant, it all made sense, and the puzzle pieces fit together. I realized my prayer to be led to service was coming true, and I had a significant role and contribution to make.

CHAPTER 8

Mom and Dad's Care

By 1995, my parents were older (Mom was seventy-two, and Dad was sixty-seven), so I rationalized this tug toward death and dying must be meant for them. Each parent, in their own right, would be a handful for any unsuspecting caregiver, so I might as well do my part and help where possible. I was being equipped to care for my parents' passing. Yes, that was it, and it felt right.

To help the reader understand the challenges ahead, it's important to know my parents, their personalities and temperaments, a little better. You'll understand why I was going to need all the help I could get.

My Dad, the Marine Clown

My Father was the only child of an accountant and secretary. Born in Yonkers, New York, he attended public school, was a Boy Scout, and achieved Eagle Scout. Later in life, he was the scoutmaster for his son's troop.

My Father loved the water and summers spent with relatives at Osceola Lake in Jefferson Valley in Westchester County, New York. It was a refreshing departure from the stifling apartment and hectic pace of New York. There was cement everywhere, and he couldn't stand it; it felt like the walls were closing in, and he needed to see lush green trees and flowing water.

My Father's Grandfather fought in the Franco-Prussian War and immigrated with his family to the United States to escape postwar Germany. His 1870 and 1871 service medals rest in my china cabinet.

My Father joined the marines at eighteen and during the Korean War was a drill sergeant and communications expert. While my Father's exact role in the marines is unconfirmed, it is suspected to be highly classified. Highlights in my memory are that he witnessed a large, cigar-shaped UFO hovering low above the Korean horizon while stationed at his communications command post. He described watching the huge shape hover for several minutes, then rise and zip away. He developed, patented, and sold the rights to a sophisticated box designed to transport classified, coded messages. A check for $700 (valued at $4,000 by 2020 standards) arrived in the early 1970s for the strangely configured box.

His role after the marines is equally elusive, but whatever it was led him to the faraway lands described previously. My Mother was always baffled why they got all the hardship posts. He retired from federal government service in the mid-1970s.

My parents divorced in 1980, and he moved to our weekend home. Because he loved the woods and water, his wallet could only afford a small cottage alongside two small lakes. He joined a local theatre group, took on roles, and began dating again. My Father loved military deception and espionage, which is why he enjoyed television shows such as *Get Smart*, *Hogan's Heroes*, *Pink Panther*, and *M*A*S*H*. Perhaps these shows reminded him of his federal employment. The community theatre gave him many opportunities to adopt other personas, which he applied with ease. Within a few years, he and his girlfriend moved to Florida. There, they graduated from a clown college, where he developed his Shang 'Hai Red the Clown Magician persona. He was skilled with sleight-of-hand magic tricks and hired by his town to provide entertainment on its pier. Cruise ships hired him for their evening entertainment programs.

When Ross Perot ran for president in 1992, he participated

in a parade in Dad's town. Desiring undercover surveillance, his organization somehow reached my Father, who went undercover as Shang 'Hai Red. Wired from head to toe, he was positioned strategically at the front of the Perot entourage and scanned onlookers for threats and disturbances. He was thoroughly entertained by the assignment.

He remained active by joining the Police Auxiliary and Coast Guard Auxiliary. I understand he was a sought-after hazardous material cleanup expert who supported spills and environmental risks in the Gulf of Mexico; a large pin with gold leaves is evidence of his national role in the Coast Guard. In my possession are thirty-nine ribbons and one medal he earned during his service between the Korean theatre, marines, and Coast Guard. He was active in the local clown and magician associations. Reflecting on his life and accomplishments, it's clear he passed down his desire to join organizations to me.

While my Father's persona softened from marine drill sergeant to clown/magician over the years, I still couldn't picture how I would be his primary caregiver. At well over three hundred pounds, it would be physically challenging to manage his care and influence him in any way. I would need help.

My Mom, the Air Force Pilot

My Mother was a majestic, strong, independent, and competent woman. She was a real head turner; at least that's what can be implied from the "Easy on the eyes" notation by her senior picture in her 1941 high school yearbook. High school activities and clubs summarized by her name include basketball, hockey, drama, baseball, French club, track and field, and newsletter staff.

One of her sisters told me that if she and their other sister were at a dance surrounded by boys, they'd turn their heads as if synchronized and say, "Who *that*?" It was their older sister entering the room majestically and yet another opportunity for her to take the limelight. The boys would apologetically dispense with the sisters, leave them puzzled and alone, and shift over to my Mother whose hazel eyes and expertly coiffed blond hair was quite fetching.

After high school, she attended a fashion and design college. She became a skilled artist and drew the tall, thin models with their fashionable hats, stiff collars, high shoulder pads, and mink stoles for newspaper fashion ads. She then worked for an extremely popular fashion house during the time, as a buyer. With varied and eclectic tastes and a love for physical activity, it's clear she'd been this way her entire life, and she wasn't finished yet.

Since 1937, the world was well aware of Amelia Earhart and her solo and record-breaking flights; my Mother was an impressionable fourteen-year-old. Reeling from her disappearance, Americans were frantic to learn her fate. By 1944, Amelia was still missing, and my Mother, like many young women, followed the news of Amelia's life, tragic disappearance, and any word of her recovered plane. Mom was a tomboy growing up, the eldest of four, and likely figured she could handle whatever the military could dish out. She was confident and tough, aware that she was smart and clever, but she never grew self-consumed with her own beauty.

In 1944, my twenty-one-year-old Mother answered the call to free up servicemen in the WWII war effort. She was one of almost two thousand candidates selected from among twenty-five thousand applicants accepted into the Women's Air Force Service Pilots (WASP), a unit within the US Army Air Forces.

She hailed from a long line of military service: her Father fought in World War I under Black Jack Pershing; she's related to six Civil War soldiers who fought for both the North and South; and her distant cousin, Peter Swallow, fought during the Revolutionary War. Not to be outdone, her thirteen-times great-Grandfather was the Reverend William Brewster, who, along with Miles Standish, led the pilgrims from religious persecution to freedom on the *Mayflower*. What a bloodline!

As she began her WASP training, she quickly identified that her favorite plane was a Stearman with its biplane and open cockpit to run support missions during the war. WASP's tasks included ferrying planes between bases, towing gunnery targets, flying repaired equipment, transporting nonflying personnel to their intended destinations, flying searchlight missions, performing flying simulations, and participating in radio-controlled flights. Her training would teach her how to perform all these varied missions. As she settled into the routines of her training at Avenger Field in Sweetwater, Texas, she got a real taste of the men's world and what they thought of the new fly girls.

One said, "Hey, beautiful! Why don't you go home and make some cookies?"

And another said, "We don't need you here. This is man's work. Go home and be a Mother, teacher, or nurse!"

The naysayers and her training were tough, but she was tougher. While I don't know her response to these demeaning comments, I can venture she used several well-chosen words as she flipped her blond head of curls, held her head high, and walked away proudly.

"No one could fly like Gen," one of the WASPs told me after her memorial service. "She knew her plane and instruments extremely well. If there was a mission to be flown, Gen could do it better than anyone."

My Mother was very proud of her time in the WASPs and the dedication and skills of her WASP classmates. "They were tough broads," she told me. "Flying was exhilarating. They came to do a job, and they did as well as any man."

The WASPs completed seven months of training, the same as male cadets. According to the WASP Museum website (wasp museum.org), they were stationed at 120 army air bases within the United States and flew seventy-eight different types of aircraft, every plane the US Army Air Forces flew, including the B-29. A total of thirty-eight women died during their service or training. Flying in her open Stearman with her well-fitting flight jacket, leather cap, and goggles, I envision her emulating Amelia Earhart, breaking through barriers and opening opportunities women enjoy today.

"If Amelia can do it, we can too," she may have said,

impersonating Rosie the Riveter's bent right arm and raised fist, encouraging the other women who weren't yet convinced.

My Mother was an excellent pilot who was impeccably skilled with her instrumentation. Formal training weeks earlier warned of flying into a strong wind, demonstrated by the stiff orange wind sock pointing straight in your direction. The severe wind shear could flip the open plane.

She was performing assigned spins, rolls, and stalls during her final exam in her trusty Stearman when the wind suddenly changed. The bright orange wind sock affixed high on its pole now pointed directly and stiffly toward her plane instead of away. Her male radioman ordered her to land on his selection of runway.

"Negative. I'm experiencing severe wind shear; request alternative runway," she pleaded.

Egos and male domination likely clashed as he responded, "Negative, recruit. You will land on the assigned runway according to my orders."

He must have thought, *Who is this lady, a recruit no less, telling me I don't know how to land a plane? She better do what I say or else.*

I picture him taking a long drag from his cigarette, exhaling, and then using mustard-yellow fingertips to crush his cigarette butt against the dusty sole of his boot.

My Mother, never shy to stand her ground when she knew she was right, overruled his dangerous order, kept a keen eye on her instruments and the orange wind sock, turned her Stearman skillfully, and landed on a safer runway of her choosing. No one is alive today who knows what transpired next between the radioman, my Mother, and the WASP commander.

My Mother told me she was "So mad I could spit tacks!" It would have been interesting to be a fly on the wall as she and the radioman made eye contact and stared each other down in the commander's office. I know the gaze of those hazel eyes! If she had been able to state her case, it didn't matter. She was dismissed and given twenty-four hours to leave the base.

The WASP website notes fourteen WASPs were dismissed for

disciplinary reasons. She certainly was one of them. How many WASPs were dismissed for false or trumped-up charges? How many, like my Mother, had no voice or recourse when they were right? Worse, how many knew they were right, disregarded their own instincts and training, and followed the men's direction to their own end?

Later that night, as the story was told to me, Mom was spotted on the roof of the training building. Her friends ran up the flights of stairs to the roof and fed her a steady stream of black coffee into the wee hours of the morning. Perhaps, in between sobs, she unleashed her feelings: "I did the right things, followed the training exactly as it was taught, and that bright orange wind sock was pointing right at me! If I tried to use his runway assignment, my plane could have flipped over with me in it! Why didn't he listen to me? Why didn't he listen? It's not fair! A simple, different runway was all I asked for. I'm a woman. OK, yes I am! But I'm more than that! I have the training, earned the right to be here, deserve to fly with the WASPs, and am proud to be part of this war!"

Her WASP sisters listened and gave her tissues as she released her feelings, cried, and wiped her eyes on her military-issued jumpsuit sleeve. About four in the morning, she collapsed, sobbing, in a heap; her classmates pulled her from the roof, gathered her up, and helped her down the stairs and back to her barracks.

Today, a woman would have an appeal process and a voice to tell her side of the story; hopefully, logic would prevail. But that wasn't the case in the mid-1940s military when a direct order was disregarded. She was escorted off the base. Throughout her life, she never fully recovered from her treatment the day of her final exam.

She must have been so proud to be accepted into this elite band of women. I picture her Father, probably very skeptical that his eldest daughter should be in the US Army Air Forces at all, let alone flying a plane. Amelia was still missing. Why do you want to do this? Then, after being accepted and doing all the work, to be dismissed under those circumstances, it was unbelievable. She must have struggled to face him. Now, here she was, expelled.

My Mother stayed close to her best WASP friends and was invited to and attended WASP reunions over the years. The sisterhood of WASPs knew and despised the wrong that was done to one of their best flyers and all the other WASPs who experienced similar fates.

Passed by Congress and the Senate, President Jimmy Carter signed a house bill in 1977 giving the WASP military recognition. Despite her alleged infraction, she received an honorable discharge and was mailed the government-issued DD-214 form. In 1979, the WASPs received veteran's status, and Mom qualified for a small pension, which was enough to pay her electric bill. The WASP sisters knew her grit, respected her skill, and knew her story. They stood by her side through the rest of her life.

After her death, one of the WASP leaders called. There was a new Women in Military Service for America Memorial opening, and she had the authority to list Mom in the directory. She said she knew Mom's story and didn't want the memorial to move forward without Mom listed. She asked for Mom's picture and a brief biography, which I compiled and sent with pride. I reflected at the dedication and commitment the WASPs made to Mom. And even after her death, they were there for her.

Mom enjoyed many years in retirement and lived in a small, two-bedroom apartment. Her normal routine involved tramping through the woods, reading, enjoying tennis tournaments on TV, and keeping up with friends and family. She had a regal style, confident persona, and pragmatic approach to life. She remained a great dresser with an eye for classic styles (think collared shirt and blazer). She was living her life and never gave any indication she was concerned about its ending. She was beautiful, tall, and slim with her shoulders pulled back, her long neck leading up to a pretty, chiseled face with crystalline blue/gray eyes, high cheekbones, and well-set white hair.

As my Mother got older, she still enjoyed fun and thrilling outings with younger coworkers and friends. She called them "the girls"; they were in their early forties when she was in her sixties. One weekend, they went white water rafting.

"There were these huge white water swells and fast-rushing water all around the raft. My safety vest was on, and I held onto the boat for dear life. One thing the instructor said was to never, ever let go of the handles in the raft," she said.

"Then a huge swell came up under us, raised the raft high, and dropped us down hard. My hand was ripped from the grip, and I toppled backward out of the raft."

This was a woman in her mid-sixties on her first white water rafting trip, and you'd think she was twenty-five.

"The next thing I knew, I was under water, flailing like a fish out of water and holding my breath for what seemed like forever. Then, the guide reached down, pulled me up by the collar, and jerked me back into the raft. It was exhilarating," she said, holding her breath, pursing her lips, and blowing the air out of her cheeks to demonstrate her first breath out of the water.

Then, there were parachute jumping lessons in her later sixties. The "girls" were given lessons on the ground before being permitted to jump.

My Mother described her jump: "It was like the old WASP days; only the equipment was better. I knew exactly how to handle the parachute, jump, soar, and land; it was so exciting to be up in a plane again." She continued, "I jumped out, threw my arms wide open, and arched my back exactly as I was supposed to. Then the altimeter connected to my jump vest released and hit me in the chin, stunning me for a minute. I landed off course in bramble bushes, was dragged by the force of the wind by the parachute, and my jumpsuit was shredded to tatters. It was great fun!"

Keep in mind this was the same lady who played tennis, took Mrs. F. to the pool, and shopped at the local grocery store, yet there was still this extreme adventurer inside! She had a lot of gusto and was fearless. I didn't get that gene. She enjoyed the opportunities afforded by the federal government during her life and posts overseas: snorkeling in the Mediterranean, Red, and Aegean Seas; shell collecting at every shoreline; fossil hunting on Mount Sinai; camel riding in Egypt; attending lavish formal events; and touring ancient Grecian, Roman, Arab, and African cities from antiquity. Her life was unique and full.

Over my Mother's life, she frequently mentioned her desire not to suffer in the end or be beholden to anyone. She knew I was a Christian and that I didn't share her views. Attempts made to engage her in discussion about the Bible or other religious topics landed on deaf ears.

With my Mother's background and independent personal constitution, she would prove challenging to care for someday. She was extremely independent and strong-willed. Yes, I would need help with Mom.

Considering what I knew about both my parents and my own knowledge and skill related to caregiving, I realized that understanding the death and dying process along with increased caregiving skills would be needed to give them the best end-of-life experience possible. I felt confident in the direction toward hospice care for my parents' and my benefit. I didn't want any regrets after it was all over.

CHAPTER 9

The Mission

Within a week, the local newspaper arrived at the end of the driveway, and I randomly glanced at all the pages, looking for something interesting to read. Turning the page to the help wanted ads, my view of the page shifted with laser focus, as if pulled to a hovering magnifying glass, directly over a small, one-inch-by-one-inch ad: "Enjoy helping others in their time of need? Hospice Patient Care Volunteers wanted for assignments near you."

I called the office, met with the volunteer coordinator, completed the application, and passed my interview. She said I would be a great fit with my experiences caring for others. By now, I was thirty-three, and it had been twenty-five years since I'd begun caring for Mrs. F. To understand my perspectives and maturity, the volunteer coordinator asked about my experiences and admired what she called my "healthy loss line." A loss line includes all experiences that one perceives as a loss. We talked about all the ways I had already experienced loss. She explained that loss equated not only to death but to other forms of loss we grieve and must process. To the prior list, we added losses from all my moves, leaving beloved people and belongings behind, changing schools, and my parents' divorce. I didn't mention my beloved patent leather shoes but secretly added them to my list.

After our discussion, she said I had experienced and processed a lot of loss at my young age and that these losses gave me the skills, awareness, and emotional maturity to be a hospice patient care volunteer. The five dreams didn't seem relevant for her to know, so they weren't mentioned. Considering the opportunity as it was described, I vowed to join for my parents and be ready when it was time for me to be their caregiver.

After forty hours of training, I felt ready and left the three-story brick building with my blue binder tucked confidently under my arm and my official name badge around my neck. The training taught hospice patient care procedures, patient symptoms, transferring a patient from one location to another, and the dos and don'ts of patient care. I learned that patients die the way that they lived, so you can't judge or try to change things you may see happening in the home. It is what it is, and it's always been that way, so now is not the time to try to bring change. It's a time to support the patient and their family. I acknowledged that I would encounter many situations beyond my control, so I would regularly pray for my patients.

Among all the messages in training, one specific recollection from a hallway conversation between another trainee and the instructor caught my attention. "No, no, no, you don't need to worry about the patient passing while you're there. That never happens. Just call the office, and a nurse will come," said the instructor to a rookie volunteer. *Whew, that's good to know,* I thought, secretly acknowledging that I wasn't ready for that quite yet. With more hands-on experiences, I knew the time would come when I would be ready. The nurse would take care of it, and that was all I needed to know.

Looking forward to my first assignment, I left the office building feeling confident and went home to wait for the phone to ring.

Relief for Caregivers

Hospice patient care volunteers give respite to the caregiver and the family while the patient dictates how they would like to use our time together.

While volunteering, I gained insight into the twenty-four-hour, seven-day-a-week caregiver experience. To do everything for someone at the end of life is a task not to be taken lightly. The patient may have some mobility or may be completely bedridden.

The caregiver plays a critical role, so their ability to attend to their own health and nutrition ensures they are fully ready and able to help their loved one. I've seen the family caregiver get sick themselves, which requires alternative arrangements to be made for the patient. Picture the caregiver in bed with a bad flu or injury for a few days. The caregiver needs strength from their hips all the way up to their shoulders: upper-body strength helps the caregiver change the diaper or move and turn the patient. It's not uncommon for caregivers to be injured in the course of working with their loved one. Common injuries include sprained/strained necks, shoulders, and backs. Older caregivers struggle with arthritic hands, hips, knees, and ankles.

Pure exhaustion can set in, and that's not good for the caregiver or the patient who relies on them for everything. Caregiving is hard work, so having a hospice patient care volunteer or end-of-life doula who can cover for a few hours a week is crucial for the caregiver to recharge their batteries, take care of their own business, and return refreshed and ready to start over again.

Unfinished Business

Caregivers are often the people who hear about desires and final wishes, but they don't always have the time to fulfill the request. To complement them, one of my favorite activities was listening to my patients for unfinished business and cues for topics of interest to them. For example, if they had half a project done, perhaps we could finish it together, or I could take it the rest of the way if they weren't able to participate. Or, if they expressed regret from the past, I tried to help ease their burden. Looking for clues in the home, it was fun to find something special for each patient. The stories that follow include opportunities where I was able to help complete unfinished business for my patients.

What follows are several of my more memorable hospice patient care volunteer experiences. Details of individuals and circumstances have been modified to respect confidentiality and privacy.

The Nutritionist

He was my first patient. He was in his early eighties and had stomach cancer. Upon learning more, he'd been a nutritionist all his life.

"Dad, this is Lauren, and she's going to stay with you for a few hours today," the daughter said, elevating her voice so her Father could hear.

"Hello, dear. Come in and sit down." My new patient kindly welcomed me.

Motioning me in with his thin hand, a now-too-large wedding band rolled freely on his left ring finger.

"I'm having a pretty good day, so let's sit, talk, and get to know each other."

This is a nice, logical introduction with nothing to fear, a nice start. Entering the pleasant living room, I noticed the telltale signs that hospice had set up the room: all throw rugs were off the floor, a hospital bed appeared in the living room equidistant between the dining room table and front-window view. Supplies such as pink sponge sticks, lip balm, ointment, thermometer, alcohol, cotton balls, and washcloths were tucked on top of a nearby bookshelf, its temporarily dislodged books stacked on the floor.

Later, responding to my patient's request for some apple juice, I noticed the familiar medicine bag on the top shelf of the refrigerator, containing medications for normal, day-to-day routines and other more significant medications for end-of-life comfort. These would be needed one day. Over the next few months, I visited every Sunday afternoon from noon to 4:00 p.m. so his daughter could visit a friend an hour away. My patient enjoyed talking about his career and beliefs about good nutrition. He reminisced often about the injustice of the stomach cancer after decades of education, service, and clean-living practices.

"Can you pray with me?" he asked one day when his abdomen felt tender.

"Sure," I said. "What would you like to pray for?" I responded, not knowing what would be important to him at this stage of his disease and not wanting to assume.

Praying with a dying person is often filled with simple requests healthy people take for granted. We'd pray for family, endurance, discernment, hopeful happenings after death, easing anxiety, to be pain-free, to sleep well, or to digest food without discomfort. He touched me one day when he prayed for my work as a hospice patient care volunteer and that my words and hands would be a comfort to others as I was to him.

As a very new Christian, holding hands and praying still felt slightly awkward, yet there was something very honest and transparent about it, and I was getting the hang of it. When you really pray from the heart, it means everything.

Cell phones were nonexistent at the time, so the daughter and I created a routine for my visits.

"I'll call you when I get there, and if anything happens, you call ahead and I'll get the message when I arrive," the daughter said.

"He'll be fine," I said. "We'll have a nice talk, and he'll take a nap later. Enjoy your break, and we'll see you in a few hours."

This was our agreement until the appointed time when the daughter returned. We repeated this routine for months. This was her chance to get out of the house and away from the twenty-four-hour care of her Dad, whose needs were growing incrementally each day.

Arriving one Sunday, the daughter said, "Dad's been sleeping a lot this week, so he may not be awake much for your visit."

"That's a big change from last week when he was awake, alert, and talkative," I said. "Did you let the nurse know when she was here this week?"

"Yes, she knows. Dad's in and out, not eating much, but doesn't seem to be in any pain; I administered his noon meds already," the daughter said.

"OK. Well, call me when you get there, or I'll call ahead if anything happens."

Recounting these communication smoke signals now seems ancient compared to the ease of cell phones we have today, but that's how it was.

"Don't worry. Just enjoy your time away," I said. "Recharge your batteries and relax."

The daughter smiled in agreement as she left and drove around the corner out of sight. I checked on her Dad, who was in fact in a deep sleep, and then went into the kitchen to put the few dishes in the dishwasher.

My patient was a cat lover with two cats. One was often walking a figure eight pattern in and through my ankles, leaving white hair behind on my pants leg. I would free myself after taking an awkward step and practically tripping over her. The second cat, a large tan and brown tabby, was instinctively timid, always in a back bedroom, and I never laid eyes on her.

Well, what have we here? I thought as the large tabby cat appeared, ignored me completely, and jumped on my patient's bed. I thought it was odd that the once timid cat appeared and now curled up beside its owner, so I felt drawn to the bedside to investigate. My patient was in a sound sleep, his chest slowly rising and falling with shallow breaths.

I took his hand and spoke. "Are you having a rough day today, dear?" I said, recalling from training that the hearing is the last sense to go. His pulse and respirations were counted and recounted to confirm his status.

"I'm going to make a quick phone call, and then I'll read Psalm 23 with you again. How does that sound?" I said, calmly patting his arm.

I then hustled to the kitchen phone. "This is Lauren Kirby," I pronounced efficiently into the phone without a hello. "I'm a new hospice patient care volunteer, and my patient is showing signs of active dying! Can you send over the nurse right away?"

"We don't have anyone close right now, but I'll send the first nurse who frees up. Remember your training," she said. It was only 12:30 p.m.

I called the daughter's destination, but she hadn't arrived. "Please have her call the house right away. We have a situation."

Returning to my patient, I was determined that the two of us were going to get through this together. There wasn't anyone else, just us and his now fully present tabby cat. Training scenarios ran through my mind as I selected a few that were applicable. His breathing and pulse were continually monitored. As I read Psalm 23, he visibly exhaled, and his breathing slowed significantly. I checked his pulse again, pulling my thumb out of the way so its own pulse wouldn't interfere. Using the remaining four fingers, I searched for the pulse along the inside of his wrist bone. I feared he would jerk awake and say, "What are you doing? Are you really checking my pulse right now?" We may recall the scene on the *Golden Girls* where Madge put the mirror under Sophia's nose and have a laugh. I checked his pulse again and noticed a light sweat on his brow and upper lip. I patted his face with a tissue. *Never while you're there*, the trainer promised confidently and assuredly that day after training. "The nurse will take care of it." My nurse was tied up, and *I was on my own*.

I prayed quickly, "Dear Lord. It's me again. My patient has all the signs of active dying, and I need help. What should I say to him? Is there something you would have me do to make this go as well as it possibly can? In your precious name, please help the nurse get here soon. Amen."

I took his hand, finished Psalm 23, and spoke softly. "It's time now. If you see a warm light, it's OK to reach for it. If you see relatives on the other side and they call your name, it's OK to answer. Everything is fine. You're comfortable. There's no pain. And you won't believe this, but your tabby cat is on the bed curled up next to you."

He passed away peacefully as I sat holding his hand. I continued to sit for a minute, processing everything that was unfolding before my eyes.

"Wow, this just happened," I said quietly to myself. "Better call the office." The call was made on the kitchen phone. Next, I called the daughter's destination. She had just arrived. I shared the news, and she turned the car around and headed home.

The tabby cat stayed on the bed until being shooed off by the ambulance crew so they could move my patient to the waiting ambulance. I stayed until the daughter arrived. We discussed her Dad's final hours and the tabby cat's strange behavior and comforted each other.

Profoundly moved that my/His/our words (and Psalm 23) were the last my patient heard on this earth left me stunned and still processing to this day. I was glad his journey was over. He died with his beloved cat at his side, and hospice met its mission of a merciful, pain-free passing. It was my distinct honor to be his volunteer, and I was hooked.

The High-Finance Executive

This sixty-something patient lived upstairs in a three-story townhouse. I was assigned the case when my patient had end-stage Lou Gehrig's disease.

One of my first tasks was to speak to the husband to find out what her capabilities and limitations were.

"Is she able to sit?" I asked.

"No," he responded.

"Feed herself?"

"No."

"Raise her head, hands, or feet?"

"No."

Deciding to change direction, I asked him to describe what a normal day was like in the home.

"We do everything for her. All she can do is lie on her back and blink. She blinks one time for yes and two times for no," he said.

"How is her mental state? Is she aware of her surroundings, and can she hear when spoken to?" I delved deeper.

"Yes, her mind is sharp, and she can hear," he said. "She just can't respond."

This was my most severe case yet. My patient was keenly aware of everything going on around her, but her system was simply not responding. I was moved by the fact that she was fully present and in there without any ability to react to anything, except blink.

I took care of her physical needs, kept her clean and comfortable, and prayed for her mental peace regularly. I talked to her and asked questions that required yes/no responses. She had a way of using her gaze to communicate more specifically to add emphasis. She still had the muscle function to raise her eyelids and give a severe look if she wanted to emphasize something really important. She would then relax her eyes for normal communication through blinking.

We spent Sunday afternoons "chatting," and I asked questions based on what I observed in her room. She and I were both in the financial-services industry, so our conversations had a natural flow. I often talked about happenings in the business, and she enjoyed listening.

"What a lovely quilt. Did someone make it for you?" I asked, walking over to run my hand over the handiwork.

One blink was returned.

"You must be much loved to receive such a special quilt, made by hands that care so much for you," I replied.

"Are these the same kids I saw downstairs?" I asked, looking at a picture on the dresser.

One blink was returned.

"Wow, they've really grown. I talked to them, and they are really nice children. You must be very proud."

One blink was returned.

My patient was diagnosed six years prior to my assignment. She was exhausting every possible avenue so she could be cared for at home. The decline with Lou Gehrig's is very slow, and I was her last hospice patient care volunteer.

When I reflect about this assignment, I am touched by her family that was trying so hard to keep the family together during this tough disease. Their love for their Mother was often all they had to give; they weren't a family of means, but they did their best. Isn't that all we can ask for?

The Teenage Candy Striper

In her late eighties, my patient would meet me at her front door and usher me to the kitchen. My patient had a rare blood cancer, and there was absolutely no one to help her at home. Family lived elsewhere, and rifts from the past impinged on lifelong relationships. After we'd gotten to know each other, she opened up about why her daughter, who lived nearby, wasn't helping her. Apparently, they had lived together, and the daughter brought home a stray dog one day. The Mother never got along with the dog, so she took it to the pound while her daughter was at work. The daughter returned home after work, found no dog, uncovered her Mother's deed, and they parted ways. I prayed for these family issues to be healed. Clearly, I'd been paying attention in my training, with an acceptance that she may well die the way she had lived.

During our visits in her apartment, she would take my hand and lead me to the kitchen and point to a wide variety of glass and plastic bottles on the counter. Knowing what she wanted, I unscrewed prescription, peanut butter, toothpaste, jelly, and pickle jars and bottles she couldn't open with her arthritic hands. On another visit, I noticed her slippers were worn and torn. We drove to a nearby department store, and she picked out a new pair of pink slippers. It only cost a few dollars, and it was worth it to see the smile on her face. Another day, I noticed she was struggling to tie the laces on her shoes. An outing to the same store solved the problem with comfy shoes with hook-and-loop fasteners.

"What's your favorite restaurant?" I asked during a visit.

She looked at me in disbelief. "Restaurant? Why, I've never eaten in one!" she replied, somewhat in disbelief that I would even ask. "There was never extra money for that!"

"Then we absolutely have to go," I said, and I put her shoes on and buttoned her sweater. We headed out.

Within minutes, we were gobbling up a hamburger, fries, and a strawberry shake at a nearby diner. Then we went for a drive in the country before returning to her home. She liked to point out neat, decorated houses with manicured lawns. These were houses that had a woman's touch with a green lawn, pretty flowers, and frilly curtains hanging in the windows. The more I learned about her marriage and level of poverty, I knew these were the types of houses she would have enjoyed had there been resources to afford them.

For the next ten Sundays, traveling to get a hamburger, fries, and strawberry shake was our routine. She was thoroughly enjoying herself and now could cite her first and favorite restaurant.

I arrived one afternoon at her apartment for a visit, and she was feeling down.

"What's the matter?" I asked.

"I'm bored and miss my plants. I've been sitting here thinking about my house plants and how much fun I had working on them when I was younger. They filled my days and gave me such a sense of joy and accomplishment." We spent this visit talking about plants and driving to get a hamburger.

On my next visit, I arrived with a box containing several small house plants, containers, and potting soil. Her eyes lit up, and she covered her open mouth with the palms of her hands.

"We're going to put these little fellows into their pots today. How does that sound?" I said, already aware that I was about to make my patient very happy.

"*Really?* You'd do that for me?" she said.

"Absolutely! Let's dig in!" I said, looking around for a good location to make a mess. We headed into the kitchen, and I put all the items on the counter.

We planted six small pots, watered them, and found a sunny spot on the floor in the living room. Then, we washed up the kitchen, had a cup of tea, and admired her creations. It was a wonderful afternoon.

On another visit, my patient said, "I'd like to be a nurse. I was a candy striper in high school, and I loved the red-and-white pinafores we used to wear."

"Wow, a nurse! That's awesome!" I said. "Did you look into it and what training was involved?"

"No, I never did." She sighed. As she spoke, I noticed our recently potted plants were now withered and brown on the floor.

"Well, I think you'd be a great nurse! I can check into that for you. Next time I come, I'll bring some material, and we can talk about it," I said, watching her for a response. What she returned were eyes full of tears and a big hug that was stronger than her little frame should have been able to give. On my next visit, we reviewed printed materials from a local university's nursing program. I also printed out some examples of what the nurses wore today, since she emphasized the uniform.

"I don't know if I can do this now. I'm older and don't really have the money, but it's nice to learn about it! I don't like the plain work outfits though. The crisp white caps, tops, pants, and shoes were much nicer," she told me as she transitioned quickly to say that her birthday was the next week.

I made arrangements with a nearby steakhouse to bring a birthday cake for our surprise luncheon (that wasn't a hamburger and milkshake). The manager said he would roust the staff and customers to sing the "Happy Birthday" song. I picked up my patient, and she thought she was going to get a hamburger. Instead, I drove to the steakhouse. My patient was confused, and I asked her to trust me. We were led to our table to find balloons tied to the back of the booth. She ordered her first steak dinner, and we laughed and laughed at the thought that she was actually eating a nice steak at a restaurant.

Then the dishes were cleared, and the waiter brought out the decorated birthday cake I had made the day before. She loved yellow roses, so I had piped a dozen of them around the cake along with a personalized message. Candles were lit, and everyone sang to her as she blew out the candles. She was beaming. We ate our cake and headed toward the door. She hugged everyone she saw: manager, customers, cashier, and waitress. I drove away that evening feeling more vibrant than I had in a long time; I was grateful for being put in my patient's life. Making a difference comes in many forms, and I enjoyed finding them all.

Within a few days of our visit, a call came that my patient was admitted to the in-patient unit of our hospice. She was in and out of consciousness and showed signs that the end was near.

That evening, I drove to the unit. Getting on my knees, I faced the bed, lightly stroked her hair, and said, "Do you remember me? We planted flowers and ate steak together."

Her eyes lit up. "Oh, it's you. You do look familiar, but I don't know who you are. I think if I knew you, I would like you. You have kind eyes."

My patient passed away peacefully in the wee hours of the morning. I volunteered a few hours at the in-patient unit working in the garden in her honor. The tulips and daffodils were just coming up, and she would have liked that.

This case helped me understand that not everyone has money to spare, and some people don't have great lives for whatever reason. I enjoyed giving her a few new experiences on our visits. By this time, my Mother was already gone, so I often thought I'd be out doing something with my Mother if she were still here. Since she wasn't, I could do for someone else what I couldn't do for my Mother. While I was my patient's hospice patient care volunteer, she gave back as much to me as I gave to her, maybe even more. And it's important to note that there's no expectation that the volunteer spend money during patient visits. This was just something I wanted to do.

The WWII Nurse

"Yes, I need to attend my painting class every week, and I can't miss it. Can you promise to be here every Tuesday at 6:00 p.m.?" she urged.

"Yes, ma'am. I can be there and will see you on Tuesday," I responded to the caregiver of my newly assigned family.

I took note of the urgency in her voice, that she needed her class and the necessity to get out of the house wasn't optional. She was caring for her eighty-five-year-old sister who had been a nurse in WWII and the year before had been diagnosed with ovarian cancer. She had good days and bad days.

"You're a what?" she asked during our first visit. "I can't hear very well, so can you speak up?"

"Yes, ma'am. A hospice patient care volunteer," I responded, showing respect for her service and hoping my voice was loud enough for her to hear me. I slowly peeked around and behind her ears to see if there were hearing aids. There were none.

"I'm going to stay with you this evening so your sister can go to her painting class," I said.

"Her what?" she asked, raising her voice.

"Painting! We can read, sing, dance, talk, play cards, or watch TV. I give a wicked foot rub if that interests you. What would you like to do?" I asked.

"A foot rub? I've never had one of those. Let's do that first," she offered. I made sure she was seated safely and then slowly took off her slippers and socks.

"I'll get a pot of warm water and be right back," I said, heading toward the kitchen.

"You'll do what?" she asked.

"Be right back," I said louder, leaving the room.

Returning with a pot of warm, sudsy water, I gave her my famous foot rub. Her initial tension eventually relaxed, and I massaged her ankle, heel, arch, and toes with the slick soap. She just watched me and said nothing. Unable to read her reaction, I moved on to the next foot. Refreshing the pot with warm, clean water, I rinsed her feet and patted them dry. Hospice always equips the bedside with lotion, so I put a small dab in my palms, rubbed my hands together to warm the cream, and slowly rubbed it on both feet. She responded with a big grin and clapped her hands. I noticed she was missing one of her front teeth.

"I want to tell you a story. Sit down, young lady," she commanded in a voice an officer would use for a private. I sat down and got comfortable. With several prior hospice patients who were in the military, I knew I was going to be here for a while. My patients were bored and had nothing but time on their hands.

She told stories about her recruitment, how her uniform was too tight, boots were too big, training was too long, and missions too dangerous. Sometimes she would share painful memories or images that wouldn't leave her. I did my best to comfort her; I prayed that her burdens would be lifted. She spoke of losing friends in battle and being wounded herself, and she showed me a large scar on her shoulder. I, in return, finding something to relate to, raised the cuff on my right arm and showed her my scar from my injury when I was four. I told her about my Mother, the WASP. Through our healed scars and WWII stories, we became fast friends.

I visited her on Tuesday nights for months. Hospice patients are usually in the program for a few weeks to a few months, but her needs were up and down like a roller coaster. The average length of stay that year was just six days. Six days doesn't seem like much, but it's because it takes time to get used to the idea that it's time to call in hospice. She was eventually released from the program because she had stabilized and shown significant improvement. In another eighteen months, she rejoined the program and passed away within a few days. I am blessed to have listened to her stories and that her sister was able to attend her class.

This case taught me that because someone is in their later years, you don't really know them. They were something different when they were young and vibrant. They had a life much different from what you're observing. As soon as I knew she was military, I always called her ma'am. I showed her respect, and in return, she showed me respect and allowed me access to her life experiences. Her military stories showed her bravery and sacrifice and how depravation in the military theatre affected her life view—simple things like being warm, having dry, well-fitting shoes, eating a good meal, having clean hair, resting, having good toothpaste, and so on. All things we take for granted, this woman lived through, and she earned my respect.

The Country Music Fan

She was seventeen with a brain tumor, my youngest hospice patient.

"Yes, sir, I will be there at noon. I have no problem if your daughter is nonverbal and disengaged. We'll be fine, and you and your wife just take the afternoon and get a break," I responded to the Father as we scheduled my first visit.

Upon arriving, the young girl was in her wheelchair. By her furrowed brow and clenched jaw, I could see that she was not happy and definitely wondering why I was there. She waved her hands and pushed her Mother away as she tried to offer her something to eat. The bowl toppled out of her Mother's hand and flipped onto the floor with a clatter. A second clatter signaled that the spoon landed nearby.

"Don't worry about that. I'll clean it up. You two just go on and enjoy the day," I said as I reached for the paper towels. Bending over to pick up the bowl and spoon and clean up the food, I was keenly aware of my patient's eyes on me, staring, drilling holes into my back.

I spun around in a single motion. "Hi. I'm Lauren. I'll be staying with you for a little while so your parents can run some errands," I introduced myself. Searching for an icebreaker, I noticed a familiar country star was singing a popular song on the radio. Welcoming the distraction, I said, "Oh, he's the best! He's got a great singing voice, and I love how nice he is. He's an all-around great guy."

I watched for a response, and my patient cocked her head but didn't speak. *Well, at least this is a start*, I thought.

The visit passed, and she never spoke when I prompted or otherwise tried to make contact. I putted about, looking for things to do that might be helpful to the family. I washed dishes, straightened the living room, straightened pillows and throw blankets, and wiped down the wooden furniture. My patient continued to glare at me, communicating her thoughts in her own way.

"We had a nice visit, and all's well here," I said as the parents returned.

I bid my farewell to my patient and headed toward the door. Now out of earshot of her, the Father ushered me out to the front porch.

"So, what really happened?" he asked.

"We listened to music. I shared some stories and then did some light housecleaning. She just watched me but didn't engage," I responded, hoping my response passed his inspection.

"Then she didn't throw anything at you? That's odd," he said, disbelieving my report.

"No, no, not at all. Once I talked about the country singer on the radio, she seemed to accept me a little more," I said, curious about other unsuspecting visitors who were on the receiving end of thrown objects or food.

"Aha! That's it! You stumbled onto her favorite country music star, and she found that in common with you!" he said excitedly.

"Oh, that's her favorite? Well, I know the star will be at a music venue nearby in a few weeks. I heard an ad on the radio. Let me make a few phone calls and maybe we can get your daughter there."

"No, that's not possible. She's very weak, and I wouldn't want to risk it," he responded with a disappointed tone, thinking the opportunity had long passed.

"Well, there are other ways! Let me see what we can do. I'll be back in touch with you soon." I left.

After calling the venue and explaining who I was and the situation, they put me in touch with the production company. Then the production company confirmed the star would be willing to have a phone call with my patient. The production company made the arrangements directly with the Father, and the call happened on time, as scheduled.

"I can't believe you pulled that off!" the Father told me. "You actually got the star to talk to my daughter. Now, he did all the talking, but I could tell my daughter recognized his voice and was so happy."

Within a few days, my patient passed away peacefully. It was my extreme pleasure to give this gift to my patient. I prayed this phone call gave her some peace and pleasure.

This case was tough because my patient was the same age of one of my sons. I related to the parents and what they were going through. I showed them my concern and gave them my very best— all things I would want if it was my child. I have nothing but respect for her and her difficult journey. It was my honor just to be with her and show that I cared, with no expectation of anything in return. She cocked her head in acknowledgment once and didn't throw anything at me. That was enough for me.

Returning to Work

Returning to work after being a hospice patient care volunteer over the weekend can be difficult. There was the usual "How was your weekend?" chatter as each employee described their days off. One person went to their son's baseball game, and another got their car out of the auto body shop. All routine topics we discussed every Monday. I would share mundane activities but never mentioned hospice. Only a few close friends knew about my hospice work, but they never received any specific details.

Another was "What did you do last night?" Common responses were dinner with family, laundry, watching TV. Sitting at the bedside of a hospice patient just wasn't what most people did or wanted to do. For me, it was a sacred space where I enjoyed being.

If I joined the Monday-morning chatter, I could envision how it would go:

"You do what on your days off?" they might ask.

"Hospice patient care. I help people who are at the end of their life. I stay with them so their caregiver can have a break."

"Huh, go figure," they might say. "Now, why would you want to go and do a thing like that? I mean, doesn't it make you sad? I mean, I can think of all kinds of things better than *that* to do on my days off."

To answer the question, no, it didn't make me sad per se. Yes, it made me happy to be part of such an important time in someone's life and make a difference in the moment. What would make me sad is if the person wasn't given proper pain management or if the medical team wasn't top-notch. Suffering makes me sad.

Each hospice visit is unique and meaningful. My hospice patient care volunteer role has been one of the most profound accomplishments in my life, with the exception of giving birth to my two sons.

CHAPTER 10
Memories of Dad

My last memory of seeing my Father was when my youngest son and I visited for a few days in February 1997. It had been a few years since we'd seen him, so we took in the experience, not knowing when we'd see him again. We toured the pier where he performed as a clown magician, and I watched my son climb the bright orange lemon and orange trees in his front yard. His time in the trees was cut short by large black ants marching up and down the tree in single-file rows. Our leisurely evenings before going to bed were further disturbed by large black (clearly prehistoric) two-inch-long palmetto bugs sauntering across the floor, their abdomens waddling from side to side as they crawled. These bugs returned memories of large African bugs, grown large due to the climate. The thought of a palmetto bug on my bed or climbing on me was too much, and I slept lightly, swatting at unseen sensations throughout the night.

The day before we left for home, we boarded a tour boat for what we thought was a short ride. After we disembarked at a small island, the boat turned and left. One of the other tourists said they would return for us in four hours. We were not prepared with hats or sunscreen. My son spotted a man selling rides on an ultralight glider, so that took about an hour. For the other three hours, we wandered along the shore, dipped our feet in the cool water, and marveled at the marine life and serene beauty. We alternated sheltering under one scraggly tree until the boat returned and deposited us back at the pier. By early evening, our sunburns painfully set in. Finding a bottle of pain reliever in the cabinet, our excitement was short-lived: its expiration date was 1993. It was 1997. A large, old aloe plant on my Father's front porch surrendered its spikey leaves for its salve. We were greasy and sticky but didn't feel much relief. I called my husband at work in the 911 center, and he read instructions from the 911 sunburn emergency card.

"Soak tea bags in hot water, let the bags cool down, and then pat the affected area," he said.

"Is there anything else we can try?" I said since it was midnight and making a pot of tea seemed archaic.

"Nope. This remedy made it to the 911 emergency card, so it must be good. Give it a try and let me know how it works out," he said.

It was difficult to maneuver the small, wet bags over the large area of burns, but the tannins in the tea indeed calmed the pain. Apart from the pre-Cambrian palmetto bugs marching with authority along the floorboard and up the wall, we were comfortable enough to get a fairly decent night's rest.

The next day as we were getting ready to leave for the airport, Dad dressed up for his clown gig at the pier. With his face painted with white makeup, eyebrows shaped, and lips meticulously outlined in red, the face of Shang 'Hai Red replaced my Father's familiar features. He kissed his grandson, then me, intentionally leaving a white smudge across my cheek as he winked, and we left for the airport. My feet were so swollen I couldn't tie my shoelaces. Hunched over and walking slowly to minimize the sunburn's pain, people in the airport stared, and a few came to ask if they could help. Being my Mother's independent daughter, I gracefully declined any help and trudged along, dragging bags behind me.

By September 1997, my Father continued to struggle with his weight and abdominal issues. A week after the world mourned the tragic passing of Lady Diana in the Alma tunnel in Paris, my Father felt unwell. Probably one of those blockages, he suspected. It was supposed to be simple, just another in-and-out-procedure. He'd had several of these procedures, and we knew the drill.

"I'm at the hospital. No biggie. I've got another abdominal blockage and will have the surgery in the morning," he said. "I'll call when I'm out of the recovery room."

During what was supposed to be another simple surgery, someone (we don't know who) authorized the replacement of the abdominal mesh installed more than twenty years earlier to introduce a new and more reliable product. This surgery was planned for the future when he'd lost one hundred pounds, sufficient to manage the anesthesia and recovery required. He'd lost thirty pounds so far, moving the scale from 366 to 333. "Portion sizes," he said. "That's the answer."

My brother had an unfamiliar intuition and flew to Dad's location. He even packed a dark suit with a misunderstood foreboding. My brother was able to visit with him in the recovery room after the surgery. The call I received was not that he'd completed his surgery and left the recovery room but that in the wee hours of the morning, he passed away in the recovery room. I wondered what impact my neighbor's prayer played in his recovery in the 1970s. He'd enjoyed twenty more times around the sun and saw his children mature and marry. He became a Grandfather to my two sons, then fifteen and ten. On the same day as his death, news outlets reported that Mother Teresa also passed away. Mom and I caught the next flight and arrived at Dad's house the next afternoon.

We organized a marine memorial service along the shore of the Gulf of Mexico with a twenty-one-gun salute and a Coast Guard service aboard Coast Guard cutters in the Gulf of Mexico. It was poignant to see the marines in their class one uniforms, so crisp and sharp. Completing a brief routine, they raised their rifles, fired, and completed twenty-one rounds. An American flag was tightly folded in its traditional triangle shape and handed to us. We left the embankment, boarded Coast Guard cutters, and sailed the required three miles beyond the shoreline for the service. The Coast Guard chaplain delivered the sailor's prayer over the loudspeakers. My brother and I held the box of ashes, stored in a tightly sealed plastic bag, and listened for our queue to scatter the ashes into the aqua-colored water. When we heard the chaplain say, "Committed to the deep," we obediently opened the box, removed the plastic bag, and shook the gray ash into the water. Environmentally friendly wreaths were then tossed upon the water. The day had been distressing, it was miserably hot, and I hadn't eaten, so motion sickness reared its ugly head. *Awesome! This is just what I need right now,* I thought.

"Landlubber aboard! We're coming in!" was transmitted over the radio, simulcast to the additional Coast Guard cutters in our party and to the shore as our boat sped toward land. Once my feet hit the soil and I got something cold to drink, I quickly recovered.

Upon returning to my Father's home and planning for how to manage his property and possessions with our living many states away, his neighbor approached me and my brother. She was my Father's girlfriend of several years, and she held out her left hand which was sporting a diamond ring.

She said, "We were going to get married, so you can have this back if you like."

My brother and I stared at each other, with no recognition that a proposal had ever been extended.

"No, please, you keep it; he would want that," we assured her.

We were contacted by the local clown and magician's associations and solicited for donations to up-and-coming performers. Apart from a few items, we were happy to let them come and take whistles, size 40 clown shoes, horns, costumes, a rabbit in a hat, colored scarves, or whatever they wanted. We parted with the saw table we had seen my Father use to saw his girlfriend in half several years earlier. (It was very convincing, I must say!) The magician's association invited us to their upcoming monthly meeting, where they wanted to honor Dad. We were asked to bring his top hat and magic wand. Two nights later, my brother and I attended the meeting, and much to our surprise, we were asked to hand over the hat and wand. The items were placed on a chair for effect, the hat tipping over the side of the chair back and the wand across the seat. He continued, "Dear Lord, may my illusions point others to your reality. May their chosen card always be the King of Hearts. Though what I do may seem impossible, let me never make claim to miracles. When I do speak of miracles, let it be of your gift of salvation and your mercy and grace in my life. Help me to remain humble in your sight, Lord, even when I am the center of attention. Let me always offer their applause to you. May any magic I do convey the wonder and joy I feel in your presence. Let this magic always point the way to you. Amen." At this point, the speaker grabbed Dad's magic wand from the chair and raised it over his head. In one swift movement, he brought it down, met with his other hand, holding each end, and smashed the wand hard over his knee. Returning the two pieces to each hand, he raised both arms over his head and pointed the two pieces at the audience. With a waving motion and his booming voice, he said, "May Bob's magic fill you all with the fun and laughter he gave to everyone as a magician." Then he put the two broken pieces together and handed them back to us. There wasn't a dry eye in the auditorium. We weren't sure what to do with the broken wand.

When we thought we were finished with services, another was proposed. My Father had been attending a nondenominational church, and his fiancée asked if we could organize a memorial service there. My brother and I both gave eulogies, and it was a fairly straightforward service until I noticed the audience. Nothing was straightforward here. Looking out from the podium, the room was full of a cast of characters. On the left side was the Coast Guard Auxiliary in their dark blue dress uniforms and snow-white uniform caps; next to them were the police in their black class A uniforms, crisp white shirts with black ties, and mourning badges. In the center were the clowns, each sporting a head with a bald skullcap, colorfully decorated hat, or wild hair and donning their unique clown persona with the addition of a light blue tear painted below one eye. Then, to the far right were the magicians wearing formal top hats, tails, and white gloves with their magic wands propped at their side. You die the way you lived, I remembered. It made me smile. This definitely was true in my Father's case, and this eclectic group of services and friends were a testament to big Bob's life.

Dad came to me in dream about a year after his passing. In the dream, I heard a great calamity and ran outside the house to see what all the noise and ruckus was about. He was driving an old, beat-up white camper with children of all ages in the vehicle, on the roof, hanging on to doors, and sitting on the hood as the camper skidded sideways to a halt. There was no sense that anything was wrong or someone might get hurt. Everyone was having great fun with a feeling they were off on a great adventure. Dad jumped out of the driver's side door and ran up to meet me in the front yard of our home. Out of breath, he said he was in a hurry and couldn't stay; he just couldn't pass without stopping to say goodbye. With that, he jumped back into the broken-down camper, waved at me through his open side window, and drove off hurriedly, with children dangling from every possible surface. He and all the children had a smile from ear to ear.

This dream was just as vivid as the other five dreams and the dream after Andrea's death. It was special that he stopped by to say goodbye and, through this frenzied and hectic scene, let me know he was off with all these kids to somewhere special. I was reminded of his time as Shang 'Hai Red and how much he grew to love entertaining all the children on the pier. I pondered why both Andrea's and Dad's dreams depicted them hurried and having to leave so quickly with "the others." It reminded me of Sandy's dream where she was hurriedly being moved along the parachute line with several others. Maybe this is another question for when I get to heaven?

CHAPTER 11

Memories of Mom

About the time Mom turned seventy, I called her apartment, and she didn't answer. I let some time go by and tried again, still with no answer. Finally, I drove the thirty minutes to her apartment to find her car in the parking lot.

I thought to myself, *This is it.*

Maintenance was called to let me in (she was too independent to give me a key), and there was no sign of her. She was known to take unreported trips to visit her brother or sister in other states or go off with friends, so I let it go. I called a few more times and still received no answer.

"Laurie, are you there?" She called on the phone days later. "I flew out to see my sister in Albuquerque and wanted to let you know I'm back."

I responded, "Well, that's nice. I'm glad you had a good time and are letting me know you're back. Problem is you never let me you were going. I called you a few times and didn't get an answer," I said, hoping to make my point.

"Did you think I was dead on the floor?" she said.

"Yes, yes, I did. I know you're independent, Mom, but I was worried sick when you didn't answer the phone, and I drove all the way over to your apartment to check on you."

About a year later, it happened again. The phone went unanswered, I drove to the apartment in a panic, the car was in the parking lot, the maintenance man let me in, and she wasn't there. This time, I turned around and went home, irritated that she was inconveniencing me like this and was so inconsiderate of me and my time. I called her the next week, and she answered.

"What's the big deal? I went over to the apartment of one of my neighbor gals, and we played Monopoly and card games. We had a fabulous time!" she said.

"That's nice, Mom. I'm glad you had a fun, but you were gone for two days. The big deal is that I was worried about you," I said, "but decided you probably went off somewhere and would show up sometime." This happened two more times, and I didn't like the feeling.

When she was in her early seventies, she started having tremors on one side of her body and double vision. Her doctor sent her to an eye doctor, who gave her special glasses to control the double vision.

"Mom, is that enough?" I said. "I mean, shouldn't someone look into the reason why this is happening? If there's double vision, giving you special glasses with inset prisms doesn't solve the problem." (My investigative skill as an auditor identifying root cause was developing.)

At one point, she was referred to an allergist who said she had allergies. Allergies? Really? We'd lived in our current state since the 1960's, but suddenly in 1997 she had allergies? She was prescribed a very strong decongestant and antihistamine, yet there were no changes in her tremors or vision symptoms.

"Laurie, my thongue is thtuck to the rooth of my mouth," I recall her saying. "I'm all dried out but thtill shaking and have the double vithsion."

Yes, yes you do. Can anyone say, "Neur-ol-o-gist"? I mean, who are the parent and the child here? Pre-HIPAA privacy regulation, I overruled my Mother and called her primary care doctor. A referral to a neurologist miraculously appeared in her mailbox within a few days. On the appointed day, we boarded the metro train and rode the short distance to the hospital where the tests would be performed.

In the waiting area, Mom said, "Can you fill out this form for me?" This was a significant sign that something was really wrong. She was an incredibly independent woman, and I'd never seen her ask for help, let alone need help to fill out a simple, one-page intake form.

"Sure, I'll fill it out," I said, taking the clipboard and unclipping the pen. She promptly passed out and listed over onto my right shoulder, her head hanging, with her chin touching her chest. Startled, I shook her awake, then rushed up to tell the receptionist what happened.

"We'll get you in as quickly as we can, ma'am," she said, devoid of any real concern. It was a neurology office, so maybe a person passing out in the lobby was commonplace? Not sure about that, I noted her lack of interest and became concerned it might be a reflection of the practice in general. If this was the case, we would be leaving shortly.

Once in the examination room, Mom perched on the exam table. A tall, slim, and tan neurologist entered, and Mom winked at me when he turned his back. I could tell she liked him. *Highly likely he plays tennis too*, she might have thought. He turned back around and began his series of questions about her symptoms and dates of onset. For many, she was incorrect, so I jumped in. *Odd*, I thought. *She didn't seem to mind my interruptions this time.* The doctor completed the angioplasty and gave us the results.

"She's probably been having blackouts, seizures, and mini strokes for a long time," the neurologist said after posting the black-and-white images on the backlit x-ray screen.

"She just had a blackout in the waiting room," I said.

"Based on what I'm seeing here, I'm not surprised. She's probably had many more that you don't know about," he said. A picture of her in the car driving fifty-five miles per hours on the highway punctuated his comment in my mind.

Pointing with the well-manicured index finger of a surgeon,

he touched the x-ray images and said, "See here, we have three aneurysms, which is extremely rare. Most people don't survive the first one. One aneurysm is in the brain stem, and it's old and calcified. There's another behind the ear, and it's also calcified." He went on, "Then there's this one behind the eye. It's changing shape with her blood pressure, moving along the vein and optic nerve, and I don't like it. She must have had double vision and some very serious headaches. Did she ever mention these?"

"Yes, the double vision has been going on for about a year, but she's never mentioned headaches," I replied after the air was sucked out of the room. Mom turned her head away because she knew my hounding her for the past year was now resulting in some serious findings.

Even if she had experienced symptoms, she likely wouldn't have shared these details with me; her independence was always front and center. As the mystery began to unfold, we were getting closer to the root cause.

"What does this mean exactly? Are there options? How much time are we talking about here?" I asked, noticing that she was becoming annoyed again at her analytical daughter interrupting the natural flow of things.

Her generation tended to do whatever the doctor said, so she didn't appreciate my challenging her norm.

"This aneurysm could burst right here and now, or she could live out her life and die of something completely unrelated," he said. "Surgery is an option, so we need to discuss it."

He turned intentionally to my Mother, put his hand on her arm, looked directly into her blue-gray hazel eyes and spoke matter-of-factly. "Dear, we can insert a coil to give more vascular support at the site. Of course, you'd have a lengthy recovery and would have to learn to walk, talk, and feed yourself again if you survive the surgery. Oh, and you'd need to live in a nursing home while you recover and rehabilitate."

My Mother's expressionless face spoke volumes without a word:

she would have none of it. My Mother enjoyed another two years of relatively good health.

"Does your Mother drive a brown car?" the very masculine voice of the heavy male smoker asked on the line.

"Yes, she does. Who's calling, please?" I said.

"Your Mother is here at my gas station, asking to get her car fixed. She's hit something head-on really hard, and it was enough to flatten the two front tires and throw the car out of alignment. She doesn't remember anything."

I drove the thirty minutes to get to her and found her sitting on a wooden bench outside the office.

"What happened, Mom?" I said. She was mumbling and virtually incoherent. The car was repaired, and we managed to get her and the car back to her apartment.

Another night and another caller: "Hello. Your Mother ran into the back of my tow truck and we're here on the right shoulder of interstate. She says she didn't see me, but my truck is one of those really big trucks—you know, the ones that tow large school and metro buses?"

"Is anyone hurt? Is there damage to your vehicle?" I asked, praying it was minor.

He chuckled. "No one is injured, and my truck is fine, but her car has front-end damage."

Within a few days, the news reported that an eighty-year-old man ran off the road and into a crowd standing at a bus station, resulting in multiple fatalities and injuries. It became very clear that we had a serious problem. My Mother was still driving in this condition and refused to stay off the road.

"You could easily kill yourself and take out several other cars or a family of four in the process!" I urged her, to no avail.

She insisted she was a good driver and not bothering anybody. She didn't react to any of my reminders about her recent accidents.

She said, "I don't know how to stop driving. You work full-time and have two children. How can I possibly expect you to be available to take me to appointments or the store? I prefer to take care of myself, thank you very much, and not be a burden."

Pleas that we could make it work went unheeded. This was consistent with her strong personal constitution and desire for independence. Driving meant independence, and she couldn't comprehend not driving even if I agreed to take her for errands or appointments during lunch, after work, and on the weekends. There was no budging on the subject, so I took her to appointments whenever she would let me.

It was a hot mid-July day in 1999, one of those very hot days when the temperature reaches the high nineties by noon and the humidity reaches 100 percent by 2:00 p.m. These figures represent "hazy, hot, and humid" in the northeast region.

"Laurie, I've called your Mother several times today to invite her over for dinner, and she's not answering the phone," said Mrs. G., our longtime family friend who used to take me to her Catholic church, where I noticed everyone could take communion except me. "You should go check on her."

I responded, "She's fine. She's just gone off somewhere; she'll be back soon, so please try her again."

During this time, John F. Kennedy Jr. (John-John) had been reported missing after flying his wife and sister-in-law to Martha's Vineyard, and the nation was anxiously tracking the search and progress.

The next day: "Laurie, this is Mrs. G. again. Your Mother still isn't answering, and I'm really afraid something has happened. Please go and check on her."

I was swamped at work and trying to plan for my son's birthday party the next day. I agreed to go over to the apartment after the birthday dinner while my husband and the young birthday dinner guests went to the movies.

I pulled into the apartment's parking lot as I had done many times before, and there it was: her car in the parking lot. There was something in the air that didn't feel right, and a sense of déjà vu from prior experiences rushed in. I brushed them off, remembering how many times this had happened before. I paused in the car before getting out and collected my thoughts. *I've been here before and felt these same emotions: Where is she? What's happened to her? Has she taken off again? Will it (it being the operative word) be this time?* Putting the car in park, I walked past her car, brushing my index finger over the hood, leaving a clean trail through the dust, and noticing that the hood was cold. Walking up the three flights of stairs to her apartment, a sense of foreboding overtook me. In the depth of my being, I knew she was there. Placing my ear against the door, voices came from the television, and water actively ran in the distance. Placing my hand on the doorknob, I attempted to turn it, but the door was locked. Moving numbly toward the apartment to the right, I knocked on a neighbor's door and then explained my concern. Maintenance was called. After the maintenance man arrived, we each shared our justifications why the other person should go in first. The negotiations ended, and he lost. He placed the key in the keyhole, the latch slowly turned the tumbler, and the door clicked open. Retreating to the left side of the door, I hid so as not to see the room as the door inched opened. As quickly as the door opened, he moved his head slowly, looked with one eye, and suddenly shut the door.

"She's on the couch, ma'am," he whispered.

"Is there any chance?" I said.

He stopped me abruptly and waved his hand. "No, no, ma'am. I'm sorry."

His task now complete, he left me standing in the hallway. I turned to the stair landing, sat down on the top step, and had a good cry. Today was *the* day—*the* being the operative word. Mustering all my courage, I entered the living room and moved quickly toward the sound of water running to find the kitchen faucet gushing at full force. Turning the faucet to the right, I was grateful the drain wasn't clogged. The upper cabinet door over the sink was open, revealing a bottle of pain reliever in plain sight. With the sudden onset of a massive headache, the worst she'd ever had, I pictured her reaching for the bottle with an unsteady hand. She was likely experiencing the type of severe headache anticipated by the neurologist. She must have known she was in dire trouble because she left the kitchen without closing the overhead cabinet door or turning off the water. Now stricken by an invisible, painful force, her reaction must have been to make it to the couch quickly, where she could sit until the odd episode passed. If she'd moved left from the kitchen toward the dining room, she would have seen the phone and called 911. She was out of time, and no 911 emergency help was summoned. Perhaps she'd had similar severe attacks that lasted a moment and then passed, so she knew the drill—just as I had experienced unsuccessful trips to find her in the past. Maybe we had both been prepared, in our own ways, for this day and this time.

Shuffling to the back bedroom, I began making what was to be the beginning of scores of phone calls over the next few days. I called 911, explained who I was and the situation, and they reached my husband. He called me to say the birthday movie was over and he would head in my direction. Our youngest son was with him. I called my brother and then Mrs. G. before calling any relatives.

"Yes, I came over, and she's here," I said to Mrs. G. I explained the scene as I found it.

"I knew it, I knew it, I knew it!" Mrs. G. cried. Then we both cried.

My supervisor was well aware of my concerns about Mother's health in recent months, and I called her next.

"She's there? Why are you calling me right now?" An audible gulping sound came from my supervisor's side of the line. "Work isn't that important."

She was one of my best supervisors, and her kindness and sympathy showed during this call. I knew the call to my supervisor wasn't important, but calling now was one less thing to worry about later. If I forgot to call, I'd be in a different kind of trouble that I didn't need.

"I'll keep you posted and get back in the office as soon as I can," I said.

This was day three since Mrs. G had first alerted me. This *third day* kept popping up in different ways. On this day, the news reported that debris from John-John's plane had been found in the Atlantic Ocean. Somehow, it occurred to me that he was a flyer just like my Mother. The news mentioned that his skills weren't sufficient for the conditions he encountered and that he must have lost his horizon line (the junction point where the sky separates from land or water). Several times in my life, my Mother mentioned that losing the horizon line could result in the pilot's confusion between where the sky, land, or water is. You may fly upside down or think you're flying into the sky, but you're actually heading right into the ground or the water. In order to manage these technical intricacies, the pilot must expertly know how to read, interpret, and trust the airplane's instruments.

My husband arrived, and our son stayed outside the building on the front steps. Planning to stay just until Mom was moved, I assured my husband I would be home in a little while. He and our son left for home. As during my miscarriage and many other calamities we've experienced since, I am forever grateful to my husband for his help that night.

The police arrived, asked questions about who I was, why I was there, the chain of events, any preexisting conditions, and concluded we weren't standing in a crime scene.

"Are you taking her?" I asked.

"No," they said. "The fire department will have some additional duties and will handle it from here." Then they left.

Shortly afterward, the fire department arrived. Similar questions and inspections ensued. They took an additional step to remove prescription bottles from her bathroom cabinet and checked the kitchen cabinets for any additional medications. Then they placed the medications in a plastic bag, sealed it, and got ready to leave.

"Whoa, whoa, hold on!" I said. "Aren't you taking her?"

"No, ma'am. She doesn't meet the criteria, so we're turning her over to your custody now. You can call a funeral home to come pick her up."

"Criteria? What criteria? She's passed away. Isn't this criteria enough?" My questions overflowed. "Custody? What custody? My custody?" *Get control of yourself, calm down, and think.*

Both the police and fire departments abandoned me. Stunned doesn't come close to how I felt in that moment. I was right back where it started—just the two of us in the apartment. By now, it was well after midnight, and there weren't any funeral homes open.

I walked back to my Mother's bedroom, closed the door, and sat on her bed in an unsuccessful attempt to calm down and collect my ragged thoughts.

There was a funeral home in our hometown where we'd attended many services. It will be the one that will manage my and my husband's services. After dialing the number, a pleasant voice said they were sorry for my loss.

"We'd be happy to help, but there's no one on duty right now. The drivers don't come in until 9:00 a.m. We'll assign a driver to get there as soon as we can. Just sit tight."

"Lord, can this get any worse?" I raised my eyes and the question to the heavens.

I didn't know how to stay or how to leave. People just aren't equipped to handle this type of situation, and I couldn't believe I was being put in this cruel position.

Sit tight, whatever that meant, was my only option. I sat on Mom's comfy, well-made bed and looked around. The room was organized and neat; it smelled like her. I recognized several family heirlooms, which are now in my possession: her great-Grandmother's cane-back chair and walnut dresser filled with dozens of Mom's soft, brightly colored turtlenecks.

At some point, merciful sleep set in, removing me from the sad setting. Awakened by the telephone ringing at about eight thirty, a gentleman's voice said, "We're on our way to pick up your Mom, missus. We should be there in about an hour."

Two gentlemen entered the apartment, each dressed formally in black suits, white shirts, black ties, black, shiny lace-up shoes, and stark white gloves. Mom would have appreciated their formality and show of respect. The men completed their task efficiently, tipped their hats to me, said, "I'm sorry missus," and then the trio left the apartment.

This scene better matched what I'd seen on television and, in the midst of this chaos, at least provided some sense of familiarity. The first phase of this ordeal was now complete.

Over the next few days, arrangements were made for her cremation and memorial service. I returned to the apartment to inventory its contents and discuss next steps with my brother. Along the wall of a back bedroom, bottled water, canned food, toilet paper, and other supplies were neatly stacked in preparation for the end of the world with Y2K. Mom felt very modern that she understood the impending technical calamity and was trying her best to prepare for the mass technology outages due to strike at 12:01 a.m. on January 1, 2000.

Based on the list by her chair, containing names such as Sampras, Graf, and Navratilova, she was tracking tennis games, likely qualifying rounds for the US Open tennis championships. Her writing was legible at the top of the list, but the letters grew shakier and scribbled farther down; the last entry was illegible. Clearly, she'd been declining over several hours, but I was comforted knowing that she kept up the fight and watched her beloved tennis games. The contents of her purse evidenced her last earthly movements on July 14: a bank withdrawal receipt, $100 in crisp ATM-generated bills in numerical sequence, and a receipt from the grocery store. Against all urging, she'd been driving right up to her death. The yet unexplained third-day scenario presented itself again. While there was no dream this time, she was found on the third day after Mrs. G's failed attempts to reach her and call to me.

There had been several dry runs over the last year revealing how my finding her would unfold. I'm grateful for the conditioning and readiness each provided and that my work with hospice provided some familiarity with the death process. Consistent with the other dreams, I was given insight through previews of actions and emotions. I was somewhat prepared to find my Mother. What were the similarities and differences? What were the causes and effects?

I smiled, recalling my Mother's regular annoyance at my analytical abilities and questions that routinely interrupted her train of thought. I let it go.

Hospice provided a certain level of training, experience, and personal fortification, but this was still my Mother. Flowing uneasily between logic and emotion, it was difficult to process everything that was happening. By the time she passed, I was thirty-seven and had been a patient care volunteer for four years.

After all this time, my Mother remains nearby. Her favorite perfumes became mine. Her many pieces of jewelry, along with her predecessor's black onyx earrings, adorn my earlobes. Her scarves and pins now rest on my shoulders.

In retrospect, while it took time to process not only the loss of my Mother and how I found her, it's clear the chain of events unfolded as they were intended for her. She was independent and able to maintain her autonomy as she aged. While I didn't have time with my Mother in the end, I wouldn't trade her swift passing for more time if it meant pain or misery for her. And I know that's not what she wanted.

For her memorial service, her military DD-214 discharge form authorized a flag-draped coffin. My brother and I gave eulogies, and stories were shared from the audience. A young man with whom she often played tennis wept openly. She probably would have appreciated knowing what she meant to him.

In 2010, the press announced that the WASPs were awarded the Congressional Gold Medal for their service during World War II. I inquired with the WASP organization about getting the medal posthumously for my Mother, and the request was denied. "But she has an honorable discharge," I pleaded to no avail. I wrote my congressman, who made further inquiries through the WASP museum at Avenger Field in Sweetwater, Texas, and Texas Woman's University in Denton, Texas, where WASP records were stored. He wrote back letting me know my Mother had been released from the WASPs for insubordination, and the medal was not a possibility.

This felt like further injustice. Disappointed, I rationalized that I'd exhausted about every avenue at my disposal.

A few years later, I attended a women's event at work. The main event was a film about women flyers and a group called the Ninety-Nines. This group was Amelia Earhart's initial women's flying group, consisting of ninety-nine female flyers. Apparently, the male pilots had an annual flying contest, and it was only for men. So the women started their own group with ninety-nine members at the beginning. This group of women flyers have maintained teams and flown their annual competition ever since. My coworker and friend was the keynote speaker at the women's event and main character in a film documentary. The film was shown, and she closed with a request for funding to help defray the cost of the upcoming competition. While I pondered what amount I wanted to donate in Mom's honor, it occurred to me that I'd seen "Fifinella" patches on one team's jumpsuits! "Fifi" was the WASP's mascot, designed by Walt Disney himself. As my friend and I discussed a donation, I inquired about the Fifi on the jumpsuit. She asked what I knew about Fifi, so I told her Mom's story.

"This isn't right, and something has to be done," she said.

She turned over every possible stone to see what happened and why Mom couldn't get the medal. She was visibly moved by the story and injustice; her wheels were turning. We met for lunch a few times, and the unsuccessful attempt through my congressman made us both angry. Mom had an honorable discharge, after all. My friend and colleague invited me to speak at the upcoming Ninety-Nines' banquet to kick off the year's flying competition. I was humbled and agreed. My husband and I attended the event and had a wonderful meal. Called to the podium, I collected my thoughts and approached the podium where my friend greeted me formally. Sharing Mom's story with this audience was very difficult because these flyers understood how my Mom must have felt; they tried to process the injustice and were disappointed that the congressman couldn't successfully appeal Mom's case to obtain the medal.

My speech wrapped up, and the Ninety-Nines gave a lively

standing ovation for me and Mom. I thanked them for inviting me and turned to return to my seat. My friend stepped forward and asked me to stay at the podium. She presented me with a Fifi pin, and I could barely keep myself together.

Then she reached under the podium and into the shelf and retrieved a small package. She then presented me with a deep velvet blue box that had some significant weight to it. I opened the box slowly to find a Congressional Gold Medal! Everyone in the room clapped and cried again. She went on to tell me that she was honoring Mom during the annual Ninety-Nines' flying competition, which was to begin the next day. She had "This one's for Gen!" printed on her team's T-shirts and as a sticker, which she affixed to the side of her plane.

Then a woman rose and came to the podium to greet me. She was introduced as the WASP Museum executive director, and she invited me to the WASP museum in Sweetwater, Texas, to share Mom's story at an event they called the homecoming. The museum was near the site at Avenger Field where Mom trained and washed out. My dear friend had managed to turn this awful story into one of such redemption and joy. It was amazing. Wow, what a night, and what a great friend I have! I am truly blessed! I knew Mom would be so proud of how her gals, who had the same grit and fearless determination as they had in 1944, came again in 2018 to her aid. The evening and heartfelt outpouring of love released a healing glow over Mom's entire situation. While Mom wasn't physically there to receive it, hopefully the energy reached her spirit. Perhaps her healing could also begin now in earnest.

During the evening, I was introduced to several film producers who were undertaking a documentary on the WASPs and were interested in Mom's story. While intrigued with the plot's twists and turns, there was a concern that no eyewitnesses were still alive or able to give their firsthand account to corroborate what happened. With this, the documentary was produced without Mom's story. Perhaps I've spent so much time describing Mom's story in this book so it can come to light. With her story told, she can be exonerated and now be at peace. "You were right, Gen!" *There, it's finished.*

The medal is now displayed in my china cabinet, and Fifi sits in my jewelry box, ready to adorn my lapel. Mom's story should help women appreciate the fact that they now have a voice, earn respect, and can move an appeal forward. Mom was denied this due process. Books, stories, and legacies need to continue to be told so they aren't lost. Something that was so very painful for my Mom ended with great joy and recognition of her experience. There's no shame in that. The Ninety-Nines came alongside her seventy-four years later and nineteen years after her death. She was redeemed, honored, and much loved that evening; what had once been taken away was restored—unfinished business, if you will, that my friend and I were able to resolve. Hopefully, Mom will view this as a positive expression and one that will replace any form of shame she may have experienced.

My Mother remained an atheist throughout her life, and I never heard her speak about her faith, heaven, or the large-print Bible I'd given her. Hopefully, in her final moments, she found her faith and was whisked to heaven, beyond the horizon line and the stars. I sure hope so, as she would enjoy the ride through familiar clouds and seeing the earth from thousands of feet high, as she once did in her trusty Stearman, its open cockpit allowing the wind to kiss her fresh face. I picture Mom being visited by a familiar, loving voice.

"Gen. Gen. Gen! It's me, Mom," her Mother may have whispered softly in her ear. "Wake up! Wake up! It's time!"

Groggy, she may have collected herself and said, "Huh? Time for what? Am I alive?"

"Well, yes and no—it's complicated. Listen, this is important, and I want to pray with you. Lord, you know Gen. You counted the hair on her head. Throughout her life, she hasn't accepted you or believed, for whatever reason. Now, her life is over. Will you give her one more chance? Will you please reveal yourself in a mighty way so she can understand? Amen.

"Gen, will you believe? Will you join us in heaven so we can be together again? Please don't let this last chance pass you by!" her Mother may have pleaded.

How she responded is a mystery. There isn't anyone alive or in this realm who knows her response.

I coined the term *twilight* to describe what happens in this fraction of a moment when one last opportunity to believe is granted before passing over.

With my Mother's and Father's sudden passing, I realized that I'd been provided yet another scenario to add to prior experiences. Both of these were very sudden and unexpected; Mom and Dad didn't have notice or time to communicate with loved ones. At the time, this was a really tough thing to handle. That said, in the end, they didn't linger and suffer, and this is the trade-off I just have to accept.

Taking this in, I realized the previous death scenarios covered a pregnancy not meant to be; two where the subjects were accepting and ready to crossover; one where the subject was young, vibrant, and in denial; and one where the subject was older, terrified, and in denial.

Reflecting on each of these dreams and my parents' own sudden passing, all the possible scenarios were covered. My training, awareness, and exposure had been made complete for a life of service.

CHAPTER 12
Purpose Confirmation

It's clear my moving into hospice care was never intended for my parents. My parents' journeys were planned and unfolded throughout their lifetimes as they had been intended. Their sudden passing caused me to struggle with my purpose and question if I should continue as a hospice volunteer. I believe that I was being groomed from the age of four by being cared for, at the age of eight to care for others, and at the age of thirty-three to follow the dreams and begin hospice care, where there is great suffering. After putting the puzzle pieces together, it became clear where I was supposed to serve. I prayed, and the answer came. For whom I was to do this was never defined; I made the assumption it was for my parents and put boundaries around it. I put it in a box. After some soul searching and praying, my gifts and mission became very clear, so who am I to set them aside?

CHAPTER 13

The Journey Continues

M y work was always for the greater good, the largesse, for the community at large. The box I had applied defined only my parents, but that was never the plan.

Over time and after helping many families in both official and unofficial capacities, my work has evolved. To reach larger audiences, training workshops were created to help demystify the stigma of hospice. The goal was to alleviate fear and make the call to learn more about the program. Fear can only be eliminated through education, so my workshops moved out into the community. My mission has evolved and grown from hospice patient care volunteer to end-of-life doula, a much broader role. The doula is a family liaison who provides education, patient advocacy, respite care, and partnership with the caregiver and family. Just as a birth doula assists at the beginning of life, an end-of-life doula supports end of life in whatever shape or form that takes, whatever the needs are.

In helping alleviate fear in others, my work has helped me understand my own life journey and eliminated my own end-of-life fears. I am bolstered with the knowledge that there are experts who can help my family at my time of need.

If you don't have a belief system, I hope my story will help you begin. In your final moments, if you still don't have a belief system,

I pray you're visited by a soft whisper that offers another opportunity to believe and cross over into the next realm. If I've learned anything through my journey, it is that *powers*, regardless of their label, do work in mysterious ways.

When it's my turn, I hope to cross over from one side to the other, over the water, through the light, into the arms of my own family on the other side, to be welcomed as a good and faithful servant. Until that time, I will continue to fulfill my calling to ease suffering and the difficult burden of the caregiver. Mrs. F., I hope, would be proud of what she set in motion so many years ago.

— CHAPTER 14 —

Epilogue

First and foremost, I wrote this book to raise awareness. Through my story and hospice experiences, I hope readers have gained insights for approaching the end of life, knowing there are experts available to make the experience pain-free and merciful. The word *hospice* alone can invoke fear and reservation, but a new focus on palliative care is changing views from fear to pain-free comfort at end of life. But don't let the word keep you from initiating a consultation and leveraging this special service or palliative care needed. You don't have to wait for the doctor to call; you can make the call. There are experts in hospice and palliative care, as well as end-of-life doulas who have literally seen and done everything. Their toolbox is full, so please don't be afraid. With this help and partnership, you can get to the finish line with no regrets and wonderful memories. You can reach me through the Contact Us on www.previewtodestiny.com if you would like to talk with me or request an opportunity to discuss the book or share my testimony.

My journey has been so unique. I wanted to document all the mystery, twists, and turns and leave an artifact for my family and future generations of my *Mayflower* descendants.

Through my work, my faith and belief system strengthened. I became a stronger and better person because I deployed my gifts and abilities in my professional career and through volunteering. When you're in alignment with your gifts and abilities, it's meant to be and you're the happiest.

My time spent in patients' homes and at their bedsides revealed aspects of the human experience no one can comprehend unless seen up close. In some cases, my face was the last face my patient saw, my voice the last they heard. I've come to realize how often we go through our days without appreciating how fortunate we really are. When you spend time getting to know people who are counting their days, your perspective and priorities change. When you put your hands on them in the course of their personal care, you see how fragile we all really are.

The dreams were recorded first because I didn't want to forget all the vivid details. Over a period of ten years, I picked up and put back down the manuscript many times. Decades are passing quickly now, and I'm no longer a young girl, so I decided to finish the project during a sabbatical during the COVID-19 pandemic in early 2020.

With a Granddaughter now, I wanted to document my story for future generations. In my possession is a 1909 hard copy book published by my great-great-Grandfather, who documented my lineage up through my Mother's line. In it, I followed clues to confirm my lineage to a Revolutionary War soldier, the religious leader of the *Mayflower,* and six Civil War soldiers. One day, maybe my descendants will hold this book and read about the marine clown and the WASP, the hospice lady, how to pray, how to find your authentic gifts, and how to serve the greater good.

The experiences are real and unique. They are mine and mine alone. Readers who recognize certain stories may have their own memories; views of any circumstance vary, and everyone is entitled to their own interpretations and views.

My final prayer for this book is this: "Lord, please use this journey so others know you communicate today just as you have always done; we just need to listen and act. Take these words to those who are facing loss, death, and dying to give them encouragement, strength, and the reliance on you. You brought them to it and you will carry them through it. You counted the hair on every head. Ease the burden of those who are caring for those who enter the dying process where there is great suffering. Amen."

ABOUT THE AUTHOR

Lauren Kirby lives in Virginia with her husband, Pete. They have two grown sons and one Granddaughter. Lauren enjoys being a Mother and Grandmother and writing, editing, and crafting. Her professional career spans forty years in business, operational risk and audit management in government contracting, and the financial-services industry. She is a member of the National End-of-Life Doula Alliance (www. nedalliance.org) and provides end-of-life advocacy, education, and patient care as an end-of-life doula. She is a life member with the Vienna Volunteer Fire Department Auxiliary, past president of the Centreville Volunteer Fire Department, and past secretary of the Virginia State Firefighters Association. She is the recipient of the Lifetime Achievement Award by Women in Technology, Nice Guys Award by Acacia Mutual Insurance, and multiple business, fire department, and philanthropic leadership awards.

Visit our website at www.previewtodestiny.com and follow us on Instagram @Preview To Destiny. Read the book, and then join the Preview to Destiny public group on FaceBook for pictures and discussions.